To Michey

The Nazis

- Through the Eyes

of a Child

**The autobiography of a young Jewish refugee
who came face to face with Hitler**

Margarete Mendelsohn

With best wishes

from

margarety

First published in the UK in April 2012 by MyVoice Publishing

Published by: MyVoice Publishing,
Unit 1,
16 Maple Road,
Eastbourne,
BN23 6NY

ISBN: 978-0-9569682-8-9

Dedications

I wish to dedicate this autobiography, 'The Nazis - Through the Eyes of a Child', to my parents Alfred and Selli Mendelsohn and to my loving family, mainly my two sons Simon and Jonathan, without whose help, support and contributions I would not have had the confidence to put all of this on paper.

They helped me recall and collate all my experiences, and Simon has spent many hours typing – and retyping - the manuscript.

Another big 'thank you' is due to Simon for giving me the perfect 80th birthday treat by taking me to see Andrea Bocelli, one of the world's greatest opera singers, perform in Glasgow, and meet him in his dressing room! I would like to have a copy of this book produced in Braille and present it to Andrea. I am sure he would understand how I feel because he comes across as a very compassionate person. But I also have an entirely selfish reason, it might give me the chance to hand the book to him in person, thereby meeting him again!

I am also grateful to my two other children, David and Francesca, and my two grandchildren, Amy and Michael, for their interest, support and encouragement in writing this story, including David's help proofing the final draft.

My thanks, too, to former Fleet Street journalist and author Tony Flood for providing additional factual material for my autobiography and editing it so sensitively, and to publisher Rex Sumner of My Voice Publishing for making the production of this book possible.

I met Tony and Rex through BBC Radio Sussex to

whom I am extremely grateful for initially enabling me to tell my story on air – through one phone call!

Radio Sussex had asked for people to ring in to reveal any experiences that may be of interest to their listeners. So I told them about my life as a child in Nazi Germany.

They sent a young man to interview me and he was so moved by my story that he returned to the studio in tears. Presenter Jenny Day then asked me to do a recording and this resulted in me given five daily slots to tell my story through interviews with Sarah Gorrell.

Sarah told me that her husband's father was one of the troops who liberated Auschwitz. The sight of the human skeletons amongst dead bodies, and the general debris surrounding them, traumatised these troops so much that it gave them nightmares.

Review By Tony Flood

It has been an honour to edit this amazing autobiography, 'The Nazis - Through the Eyes of a Child', for Margarete Mendelsohn, whose bravery, determination and faith, in both her parents and her religion, enabled her to cope with the horrors of the Holocaust.

As she says, she will always be haunted by the atrocities inflicted by the Nazis. She still has recurring nightmares of the way six million of her fellow Jews were persecuted and murdered by the Nazi regime.

Helping to research additional material for this book has given me a much bigger insight into how Jewish people like Margarete suffered new traumas after the war ended. It was only then that those who had fled to England found out how many of their friends and relatives had decided to poison their children and then themselves, rather than be thrown into concentration camps.

Margarete and her mother fled from Berlin when she was eight years old, but she had already witnessed some terrifying events and come face to face with the world's most evil man – Hitler.

She explains that these horrors have remained with her ever since. They have caused her to suffer bouts of depression and to be repeatedly distressed by terrible memories that will never leave her.

In telling her story in this moving and gripping book she has helped to show later generations just how dreadful life in Nazi Germany was – and to ensure that the persecution of the Jewish people and others will never be forgotten.

Tony Flood – author of 'My Life With The

Stars – Best, Ali and The Panties' and 'The Secret Potion'.
www.celebritiesconfessions.com and
www.fantasyadventurebooks.com

CHAPTER 1:

FACING THE WORLD'S MOST EVIL MAN

Even now, 74 years on, I still shudder when I think back to those dreadful days in Berlin.

I will never forget, as a young girl fleeing Germany with my parents, witnessing a fellow Jew being taken off our train and beaten by the Gestapo as he lay on the platform.

Neither can I get out of my head the horror of seeing Hitler glance in my direction three years earlier. People all around us were chanting his name, but our Jewish friends and neighbours were cowering in fear.

Coming so close to the cruel dictator, and feeling the bad vibes he exuded as he drove by that spring morning in 1935, was to dictate the course of my life, it was the day when my father decided to get us out of Germany.

This was the day that I will always remember. I was only five years old, but in my mind it seems as if it were yesterday that I came face to face with the world's most evil man.

My parent's and I were with a couple of friends who also had their daughter with them. It was a beautiful Sunday morning in May and we were walking along a big wide boulevard called Unter den Linden (under the linden trees), in Berlin.

Huge trees lining the avenue were gently waving in the soft breeze. As it was usually a quiet road, I was surprised to see hoards of people standing on the pavements.

There were children, taller than me, handing out flags to people. The flags had a black background, with red writing in the middle. As I couldn't yet read, I was unable to make out what it was. I asked my father if I could have one of those flags, but he said "no." I persisted by asking "Why not?" and he replied: "I do not want you to have one."

He took my hand and said to the other adults: "I think we had better go!" At this time there were so many people on the pavements that it was impossible to get through the crowd.

I don't know why but I began to feel very uneasy. Suddenly we heard the sound of motorbikes which were driving slowly along the road. These were followed by a group of young people dressed in brown shirts, with a brown leather strap slung over their shoulders. On one arm they had a huge red band with the same picture that I had seen on the flags, a black swastika on a white background. Their other arm was raised in a salute. They began to sing the song 'Deutchland Uber Alles' which translated is 'Germany above everything'.

And then slowly, very slowly, an open top car drove by, backed by solders carrying guns. The man in the car was dressed in the same way as the people marching. He had black greasy hair, drooping over his forehead, and a short black moustache. Even as a young child of five I sensed that there was something evil about this man. He looked across in my direction with his cold, menacing blue eyes, and as they met mine, I felt an icy shiver run down my back.

It meant nothing to Hitler that he was looking into the eyes of little Margarete Mendelsohn, but it still haunts me to think about the aura of that wicked man who sent thousands of Jews to their deaths.

The throng on the pavement were shouting "Heil

Hitler, heil Hitler, our saviour," and "Down with the Jews."

I held tightly to my father's hand and said: "Please, can we go home now?"

We had a terrible time weaving our way through the crowds who were still shouting and singing, and many were blocking our way. At last we managed to get clear of this mass of excited people and, with much relief, climbed into a taxi.

My father Alfred said quietly to my mother Selli and our friends: "This is the beginning of the end of our lives in Germany. We have to move to another country to get our children and ourselves to safety." He added: "This little man, this jumped up house painter, is a death threat to all our people."

Hitler's rise to power started in the early 1930s. He was hailed a saviour and a leader after the depression which had followed Germany's defeat in the first world war which they had never recovered from economically. As in every crisis a scapegoat had to be found.

Hitler scorned anyone who didn't fit the blue-eyed, blond master race, and his ultimate target was the Jews.

Jews had been in Germany for generations. Many were professional or business people. They worked hard to look after their families and were quite well off. So Hitler led gentile German nationals to turn their wrath on Jews who lived in the lap of the land. They also blamed them in part for Germany's defeat in the First World War.

Consequently most non-Jewish people suddenly had a deep hatred for the Jews. Hitler planned the 'Final solution of the Jewish problem' and built horrific concentration camps. As early as 1933 the Nazis started sending people to these camps.

Hitler's plan to build concentration camps all over the country also brought work – and money – to ordinary German people, many of whom had been unemployed since the end of the First World War.

Initially camps were for a mixture of people who were considered undesirable, such as Jews, communists, socialists, political prisoners and homosexuals. People were often worked to death in those camps. It was later that the camps became associated with just the Jews when the Nazis planned to exterminate them as part of the final solution.

We heard through the grapevine that a very good friend of my father's, together with his wife and children, had been thrown into a concentration camp during the Nazi occupation of Belgium. I think it was Dachau. They were taken in 1941 by which time we had escaped to England.

It was terrifying for the children who were separated from their parents. Their mother and father were forced to work from dawn to dusk until they were both too exhausted to eat their meagre rations.

The wife was very attractive and the guards decided to use her as a prostitute, forcing her to have sex with a host of men. The husband was sent to do hard labour and when he could not work any more he was sent to the gas chamber.

Guards at the camps, both male and female, were completely inhuman, without a shred of decency between them. Inmates who stepped out of line or asked for a little more food were usually flogged to death.

All the old people, whom the guards sarcastically called 'mother', were herded together and told they were going to have a shower. The victims were forced to remove their clothing and put in gas chambers.

Gas, (usually Zyklon-B) was released in the room and everyone inside was dead within about 20 minutes. The ash and the smells invaded the whole camp, and the black mist of burnt humans was clearly visible in the air.

The death camps were chillingly effective as a means to murder thousands. Some camps such as Auschwitz-Birkenau could accommodate over 4,000 people at one time. Never before - or since - had there been a more systematic and brutal extermination of such a large group of people, which included around six million Jews.

It's hard to believe how far man's inhumanity to man can go because of Hitler's lust for power and desire to rule the whole world.

CHAPTER 2:

A LITTLE GIRL IN BERLIN

I was born on January 2nd 1930. I was not a planned baby - my parents had been married only one year when I put in an appearance.

My father wanted to introduce his pretty young wife to his business friends and take her with him on his trips round Germany. But having a young baby kept her at home. Even though my parents engaged a housekeeper, my mother wanted to be with me.

I was a puny baby, slow to gain weight, and for the first two weeks of my life I didn't open my left eye. When I finally opened it my parents were alarmed to see that my pupil was right in the left corner in a very pronounced squint.

Myself aged three on my grand-parents farm before I devoured carrot, earth and all, 1933.

As time went on I started to gain weight. I had a lot of black hair and began to look quite bonny. As I started to eat solid food, my nanny decided that I must eat spinach. One morning she gave me spoonful after spoonful which I reluctantly swallowed. That afternoon my mother took me to Berlin Railway Station to meet a friend of hers. While we were waiting I put the ribbon of my coat into my mouth and all the spinach came out.

When my mother's friend got off the train and came over to us all she could see was a baby covered in green slimy spinach. From that day on the sight of spinach made me ill! I think my mother sacked that poor nanny when we got home.

Life at that time was good in Berlin and we Jews

Me aged 6 with my mother in Berlin.

had no idea of the terrors and torments that awaited us, with me being traumatised when my mother was locked up in the local police station cell. But I will come to that later.

I grew up into a happy little toddler. Although I was not spoilt, I had some wonderful toys. My mother told me I was a bright little girl as I was talking fluently at 18 months.

The only bane in my life was the fact that I had to wear glasses from the age of three. Every morning when I woke up I thought of new places where I could hide them. I put them in flower pots and down the toilet. My mother and her housekeeper Grete spent long frustrating hours trying to find them!

One morning, there was some soup simmering on the stove. I got my little stool, stood on it and threw the glasses into the chicken soup! I felt sure that the glasses would melt in the hot steam. But, alas, when Mum dished Dad's portion out with a ladle, low and behold there were the glasses fully intact!

Grete took the offending glasses and put them under the tap to wash them. Both my parents insisted I wore them, but the smell of chicken lingered for many a day.

While on a business trip to Hamburg, my father walked past a very big toy shop. He suddenly had a brain wave. He went into the shop and asked them to make a pair of glasses that would fit a doll. When my father bought the bespectacled doll home and showed it to me, I was thrilled with it and decided that from that day on I would wear mine.

As an only child, I grew into a quiet, shy little girl with a vivid imagination. Until I reached the age of five, I was untouched by Hitler's awful new regime.

My main concern in the early years of my life was

about my eye sight. I envied my friends, Susie, who lived in our block on the next floor, and Gussi, the daughter of our dentist, because they did not have to wear glasses like me.

My parents took my to an eye specialist who said I should have my good right eye covered and learn to see with the left one. Reluctantly, I wore a patch on the good eye, which became more and more uncomfortable. I begged my mother to let me take it off a few times during the day. Unfortunately, that caused my eye to become lazy again, and till this day I have not much vision in it.

The best part of my life was the three months of each year when my lovely Grandma Antonia, (nicknamed Tony), came to stay for the summer.

I remember her taking me into town on the train. We looked at the other passengers and, in a whisper, made up stories about them.

Our first task was to buy Gran a dress in a smart department store. She asked a rather snooty-looking assistant to see some black dresses "with pockets," I chipped in. "Oh, yes," Gran said. "They must have pockets." Gran's pockets were a standing joke with us. Being very tidy, she put everything she found laying around the flat into her pockets and emptied them out on the kitchen table each night.

When Gran tried on the dresses, the first one was too tight and the second too frilly, but I loved the third dress. "Oh, yes, Gran, you look absolutely beautiful," I said. The dress had a lacy collar around the neck and sleeves, and hung in soft pleats down the skirt.

"We'll take this one," Grandma told the sales lady. "My granddaughter always knows what suits me." I felt six feet tall. Grandma Tony always made me feel good about myself. "Now it's your turn," she said. "I did not bring a present for you this time because you are old enough to choose your own."

We visited the toy department, where I ignored a galaxy of games, teddy bears and dolls with hair. I made my way over to the baby doll section and then I saw him. He lay in his cot, he was quite big, sleeping sweetly and his long lashes looked like fans on his cheeks. As I gently lifted him out of his bed; the baby doll's eyes opened. They were bright blue and looked at me pleadingly as if to say, 'Buy me!' So we did.

The women behind the counter asked: "Do you want the doll in the box?"

"Oh, no," I said. "I will carry him." I promptly christened him Hansi.

We then went into an open air café where Grandma bought me a glass of lemonade and a slice of bread and butter. I kept stroking the doll's face and I felt so happy that I could burst.

"You are the best Grandma in the world," I told my grandmother. "And you are best granddaughter," she replied.

I started crying a week before it was time for Grandma to go back to live with mum's sister, my aunt Martha, her husband Herman and their son Gunter, who was three years older than me and very spoiled.

I did not like staying with my aunt, uncle and cousin. Although I was happy to be with Grandma, I found the rows between my aunt and uncle disturbing.

Uncle Herman was a big, swarthy man who ruled his household with a rod of iron. He scared me and I did not like the way he looked at Mum, or how he rubbed his hand up and down my leg whenever he pulled me on to his lap, much against my will. Whenever Mum saw this she made some excuse to tell him that she wanted me for something.

Gunter was a mixed up boy. As a nine-year-old, he had enough toys to stock a toy shop. He was rude to his mother and housekeeper, and was scared of his father, who either covered him with kisses or hit him with their dog's lead.

Even though I was sad to say goodbye to Grandma Tony, I was pleased when it was time for Mum and me to go back home.

Once a week Mum and I went to visit Dad's Mum, Grandma Francisca. We had tea with her and then waited for Granddad Moritz and my dad to come back from the office.

I enjoyed playing with the big dolls house that Granddad Moritz had especially built for me. It had four rooms, electric light and running water.

I became so excited when my granddad arrived home. I remember him teasing me by saying: "I'm afraid I forgot that you would be here to day. So I've got nothing for you." This was a game we always played.

"What's that in your pockets, then?" I'd ask. As usual, when I rummaged through his pockets, I found a doll dressed in national costume and a bag of boiled sweets, a little book, and a small bag of pencils.

My granddad and I adored one another. But he died when I was seven. He never recovered from the death of his daughter Margarete, who I was named after. She had committed suicide as a result of being jilted and left pregnant by her boy friend, a great loss as she was such a lovely person and a very talented pianist.

The first time we visited Grandma Francisca after Granddad's death was a great ordeal for my parents and me. Grandma seemed quite composed, but her housekeeper Mrs. Goetz burst into tears as she greeted Dad.

When the clock struck six, I sat looking at the front door, unable and unwilling to believe that Granddad would not come through it.

CHAPTER 3:

THE SITUATION IN GERMANY DETERIORATES

The first few years of my life were really happy and idyllic. But from 1935 onwards strange and scary things were happening in our home town due to the Nazi influence.

It got progressively worse, with the result that Jewish people were shunned and barred from certain places, such as shops. We were showered with insults by the Nazis, who also threw stones through our windows and put excrement on our possessions.

It was to result in the vandalizing of hundreds of synagogues and buildings and the murder of many Jewish people.

Fortunately, none of this affected me when I first went to school, but at the end of the third term anti-Jewish slogans

Myself aged 6, 1936 in Berlin, where I started school carrying the popular Zucker Tutte

were written on the school walls and windows were smashed. Parents, fearing for their children's safety, removed them as pupils and, at the age of eight, I was taught by my mother at home. I did not attend a school again until we emigrated to England.

My parents had chosen a Jewish school for me, although it was not strictly orthodox. There was (and still I believe), a very enjoyable ceremony in schools in Germany called Zucker Tűte, with all the new six-year-old children attending for just two hours on the first morning.

On my first day at school I had arrived there with a satchel on my back, holding tightly to my parents' hands. We were shown around the building and met the teachers. When we came out our parents were waiting by the school gates, holding brightly coloured cone-shaped bags full of sweets and small toys.

After the first day I had a rude awakening. I was delegated to sit at the back of the class and found it difficult to see the blackboard clearly. My parents had told my teacher about my vision and asked if I could sit at the front, but either she forgot or just couldn't be bothered to comply with their request.

While all my class mates were getting on well with their reading, I just could not grasp the basics of it.

But this suddenly changed when my mother gave me several hours of her patient tuition. I finally understood how to read, and could not wait to go to school the next day.

When the teacher asked who wanted to be the first one to read out loud, instead of cowering behind my desk as I usually did, I shot my hand up. I stood up and read a whole paragraph without any mistakes.

"Thank, you, said the teacher, quite astounded. "You did very well indeed."

But life was becoming almost unbearable for myself and my parents.

That day, as a five-year-old, when I came face to face with Hitler as he was driven through Berlin was, perhaps, the first time I became aware of how our life was to change for the worse.

It had been such a strange experience because most of the crowd roared "heil Hitler, heil Hitler" as his car approached and some people called him their savour.

But the atmosphere wasn't right. I heard someone shout, "Down with the Jews" and my family and friends looked shaken as the little man with a big Swastika, short moustache and greasy, dark hair, swept over his forehead to one side, drove by with his arm raised.

My father's and friends' faces had gone quite pale and I heard my dad say in a quiet voice: "There is going to be a lot of trouble here." Even though I was so young, I sensed that my parents were very worried and I had felt a sort of panic about our future.

We could no longer go into certain shops and restaurants. Shops we had frequented ever since I could remember had signs in their windows saying "Juden Verboten!" (Jews forbidden).

Non-Jewish friends of Mum's, who had always stopped to chat while we were out shopping, pointedly ignored her or crossed the street when they saw her.

I was puzzled when Mum and Dad and Grandmother Tony talked together seriously at home, but stopped whenever I came into the room.

One evening Dad came home from his office and told Mum that while he was on the train two Gestapo officers spent the whole journey saying terrible things about the Jews, forecasting the dreadful fate that awaited them. They tried to draw Dad into their conversation because, with his red hair and fair skin, my father did not look Jewish in any way.

While they were talking Dad was furious and upset. When he finally got off the train he found that he had dug his nails into his hands so hard that they were bleeding.

One morning Greta received a letter and burst into tears. "I have got to leave you," she sobbed to my parents. "I am not allowed to work for you any longer." The three of us were terribly upset. I could not imagine life without her. She had been with us for four years and had cared for me whenever I was ill.

"Why must you go?" I asked her in tears. "Don't you like us any more?"

She replied: "I will always love you, but I have got to go and look after my mother, she's very ill." I did not remind her that she had told me once that her mother and father had died when she was little and she had to live in a home for children who had no parents. She always said that our home was the first one she had ever known. Now she stood by the front door, dressed in her black coat and hat, ready to leave for ever.

Dad gave her three months' wages and then she was gone. I watched from the window as Greta slowly walked along our road for the last time, a lonely figure who probably had little idea what she would do next. She had been driven out by the Germans bringing in a new law that no Christian person could work for a Jew in service.

I could not understand any of what was happening and began to have sleepless nights. When I did sleep, I had very scary nightmares. I longed for my grandma Tony to come back to us from the home of my aunt.

Dad came back from work one evening very depressed. "I have lost the company," he said. "I have got to hand over the keys of the business to Herr Smith tomorrow."

The next day my father called his staff into his office and told them he could no longer be their employer. All of the staff, none of whom were Jewish, shook his hand and said that they would not work for anyone else. My father and grandfather had been very caring bosses and had got involved in their employees' home life, helping them if they were in any financial difficulties or if there was sickness in the family.

When my father told my mum what had happened he broke down and cried like a baby. It was the first time I had ever seen him cry, and this was all too much for me, the whole of my world was falling around my ears.

"Why are you going to give the office to Herr Smith?" I asked. "It's yours and Granddad's."

Dad sat me on his lap and said: "The new German leader does not like Jewish people. He wants them to leave Germany so we are thinking about going to live in a country called England. I've got a very good friend there who wrote to me and told me he could find me a job."

I was quiet for a minute, taking in this traumatic news. The first thing I said was: "Will Grandma Tony come with us?"

"I hope she will," he said.

I could not get to sleep that night, my thoughts were jumbled. I would have to leave the flat that I grew up in. I wondered if we would take all our furniture and how we would do that. Would I be allowed to take all my toys, and, most important of all, would Grandma Tony really come with us?

Ironically, she moved in with us soon afterwards in the winter of 1937 because aunt Martha and uncle

Herman rented a luxurious flat in the smartest area of Berlin for themselves, cousin Gunter, their maid, nanny and skinny greyhound. Grandma being with us made me feel more secure.

Dad planned to travel to London in May of 1938. But three days before his departure, he caught scarlet fever. Mum managed to get a nurse to look after Dad as he was very ill, while grandma Tony and I were sent to stay with grandma Francisca.

I hated being there. I had to share grandma Francisca's double bed with her. Not only did she snore like a fog horn, she got up in the middle of the night and urinated loudly into a large chamber pot. The thought of all that putrid water swirling around the pot made me feel sick.

Dad took quite a considerable time to recover. Fortunately, the only long term side effect was that the arches of his feet dropped and he had to have specially built up shoes for support. All the time Dad was ill Peter, our canary, did not sing. Yet as soon as Dad was able to get out of bed and stand outside the door of our lounge to give Peter his usual whistle, the little bird answered with his sweet song.

My father sailed for England in early summer. Two months after his departure Mum received a letter from the landlord, informing her that Jews were no longer allowed to remain in our luxury flat, and we must find somewhere else to live. We were given only one month's notice.

Mum found a two-bedroom flat, with a balcony, opposite a synagogue. Dad was getting more and more concerned about our welfare. He wrote to Mum saying that he was doing everything possible to speed up our emigration.

Then something terrible happened. A car, driven

by a high-ranking Nazi official, crashed into Uncle Herman's car. Herman knew that when the case came to court he would be named the guilty party, even though the Nazi officer was to blame.

My poor uncle feared he would be sent to a concentration camp. The stress and worry caused him to suffer a massive heart attack and he dropped dead in the street.

When he heard about his father's sudden death Gunter had his first full blown epileptic fit.

Aunt Martha and Gunter moved in with us and Grandmother Tony, and, although we felt very sorry for them, living with them was awful.

Gunter was rude to Grandma and to Mum. He did not like to see me sit and read or play with Hansie, my doll. Aunt Martha was his devoted slave and could not see or hear a word against him, even though he would slap her face when he had one of his tantrums.

One sunny Sunday morning I needed a bit of space so Mum agreed I could take my doll Hansi in his pram and sit on a seat just outside the flat, where she could see me from our balcony.

Suddenly I was surrounded by four big boys in Hitler youth uniforms. They obscured my view of our balcony so I had no way of calling Mum for help. I was petrified and frozen to my seat.

At first they called me names, shouting: "You ugly four-eyed Jew, how dare you sit on this seat" and "This is not your country any more, you will all be in prison soon."

Then one of the thugs snatched my doll out of the pram, and played ball with him. I got up and tried in vain to catch him. After this, they kicked Hansi about as though he was a football.

One of the boys threw the doll over my head onto the tram lines behind me. I heard the smash of his china head as it hit the ground and shattered. With strength born out of desperation I pushed my way past them and ran screaming up stairs. I was so incoherent that at first Mum and Gran could not understand what I was saying.

I lay on my bed all that day, not eating or drinking, my chest heaving with dry and painful sobs. Mum and Gran sat gently wiping my burning face with a cold towel. Occasionally I fell into an uneasy sleep, waking in a cold sweat, thinking I was still on that seat surrounded by my tormentors.

The next morning Mum took the body of my headless doll to the best toy shop in town, ignoring the sign saying "Jews not allowed", and had a new head put on it.

When she returned she said to me: "Look, darling. The clever lady in the shop managed to mend your dolly's head."

I looked at my doll and knew at once that this was not the old head, from which bits of paint had been missing.

"I don't want it," I blurted out. I was about to refuse to accept the doll until I looked at my mother. Her eyes were anxious, and I remembered how she had sat with me all night. In that instant I became the mother and she became the child. I took the doll from her and managed a watery smile, the first in 24 hours. "Yes," I said, "The lady in the shop was clever."

A few weeks after this awful experience I became ill with a mild case of measles. Two weeks later Mum came down with it. She was so ill that our doctor suggested to Gran that she should hire a nurse. He told Gran that he knew of a very competent nurse, who was no longer allowed to practice simply because she was Jewish.

She arrived the next morning and I hated her on sight. She was very fat with an appetite like a horse. Poor Gran spent most of every day in the kitchen, making tasty meals for her.

The nurse also had an unnatural obsession with her digestive system. Whenever she went to the loo, she came back into our lounge, rubbing her stomach, saying, "That's better, I had a very good movement!"

She was, however, an excellent nurse, and got Mum through a very serious illness. Before the nurse left she decided to take me in hand, making me walk around the room with a book on my head in order to improve my posture. She also told me that she knew for a fact that children who sucked their thumbs were not allowed to go to England. Although I was eight years old, I still sucked my thumb, having previously held an old flannel which I rubbed over my chin. It gave me some comfort after the stress of all that had happened around me.

When she told me this, I stopped sucking my thumb immediately. But I began to nervously blink rapidly and twitch with my face. This was a habit that followed me into adulthood when tense or distressed.

It took Mum a long time to get her strength back. In order to make herself feel a bit better she decided to go the hairdressers. The girl who washed her hair informed Mum that she had a big bald patch at the top of her head.

The manager of the hairdressing saloon said she knew of somebody who could help. He was known as the Wasserman, (Waterman). Although his treatment was quite unorthodox, he had great success with problems like this.

He duly arrived the next morning, carrying a jar full of creepy crawlies that looked like frogs or tadpoles. He told Mum to put all the reptiles on her head every day for a week and assured us that her hair would grow back. Much to our surprise, he was right!

Mum was extremely worried about our dwindling finances and the dangerous situation in Germany. One morning she received a letter from the local police, asking her to attend the next day. She was still weak from her recent illness and shaking with fear as to what the police could possibly want.

She reported to them at the stated time and had to stand for one hour before a sergeant decided to see her. He told her that my father had broken the law by not telling them that he had no intention of returning to Berlin. As his wife, Mum was responsible for his actions so she had to spend two nights in the cells. She was allowed to make one phone call.

Mum rang Gran who immediately telephoned our solicitor, a non-Jewish German called Rabou. He dashed to the police station and, after pleading Mum's case, managed to get her imprisonment reduced to one night instead of two. Rabou went to meet her the next morning and signed the relevant papers for her release.

I remember asking Gran that night where Mum was. She told me she was staying with a friend. But looking at her worried face, I didn't believe her.

Suddenly I went into a panic thinking something horrible had happened to Mum. I was really relieved when she arrived home the next morning, looking very pale.

CHAPTER 4:

A NIGHT OF TERROR, VANDALISM AND

MURDER

Occasionally I would sleep in the same bed as my mother, which we both found comforting. We had just cuddled down together one night in November, 1938 when we heard a loud crashing outside in the street. The noise got louder and louder, accompanied by shouting and singing.

This was to be the most terrifying night of our lives, with the Nazis committing terrible acts of vandalism and murder.

We got out of bed and went into our front room where Gran and my aunt and cousin were cowering on the sofa. The sound of shattering glass and heavy stones being thrown could be heard. This was accompanied with hysterical laughter and cursing of Jews by the Nazis outside.

Eventually the noise abated and foot steps receded into the distance. We sat on the sofa until the sun shone weakly through the curtains because we wanted to make sure the street was empty of the Nazis.

Mum went over to the window and drew back the curtain. I will never forget the sight that met my eyes. The street was littered with stained glass windows from the synagogue lying in coloured splinters.

Pieces of the Torah, the book of Jewish scriptures and other sacred writings, which were normally dressed in a lovely blue and burgundy coat, lay in shreds, covered with human excreta. The delicate parchment on which the prayers and psalms were carefully inscribed hundreds of years ago were charred remains.

We could still smell the acrid smoke. The only things surviving this carnage were the golden shields which used to hang over the Torah. They glinted in the morning sunlight. We stood at the window, numb with fear and dreadful foreboding of what else the Nazis had in store for us.

This became what was known as 'The Night of Broken Glass, (Kristallnacht)'. It occurred on November 9th 1938, after 17-year-old Herschel Grynszpan shot and killed Ernst vom Rath, a German embassy official in Paris, in protest at the harsh treatment his Jewish parents had received from Nazis in expelling them from the Reich, together with 17,000 other Polish Jews.

In retaliation, the Nazis unleashed an horrific wave of vandalism. In the space of a few hours thousands of synagogues, stores, businesses and homes were damaged or destroyed, with glass from shattered window panes covering the streets.

Storm troopers burned or destroyed 267 synagogues, vandalized or looted 7,500 Jewish businesses and killed at least 91 Jewish people. They also damaged many Jewish cemeteries, hospitals, schools, and homes as police and fire brigades stood aside.

Kristallnacht marked an intensification of Nazi anti-Jewish policy that would culminate in the Holocaust: the systematic, state-sponsored murder of Jews.

For the first time Jews were arrested on a huge scale and taken to Nazi concentration camps. More than 25,000 Jews were sent to Buchenwald, Dachau and Sachsenhausen, where hundreds died within weeks of arrival.

As a kind of cynical joke, the Nazis fined the Jews

one billion Reichsmarks for the destruction which the Nazis themselves had caused during Kristallnacht.

Life was a misery for Jewish people, with travel restrictions, businesses being taken away, schools shut and general abuse and victimisation, which led to mass genocide.

Every night storm troopers and the Gestapo knocked

Winter 1935, Dad and I, Dr Hammond, Dr Mann,
my friends Gussi and Susi.

on the doors of Jewish men and arrested them on some pretext or other.

My mother felt that she had to help our best friends Dr Mann and our dentist, Dr Hammond. Both men slept on the floor, and left every morning before the sun came up, thankful that they had gained another day of freedom. If we had been caught hiding the men it would have been the end for all of us.

For three weeks they crept into our flat after dark and when I ran to greet them Mum put her fingers to her lips and whispered, "Hush!" At first I thought that it was a game, but I soon realized it was grim reality. Mum put pillows and blankets down on the floor in our hall for the men to sleep on.

After three weeks the men no longer came, and when Mum rang their homes it sounded like the phones had been disconnected. We never heard from them again. Dr Hammond was the father of my friend Gussi and so this was deeply distressing for me. I started to have nightmares, dreaming of the terrible things that might be happening to her.

Mum was finally able to organise our emigration to England. Just when she thought that everything was arranged she was summoned to the local police to have her passport and visa checked.

She again had to wait for a long time while other people who had come after her were seen. At last her name was called and she stood in front of a policeman for at least another hour. When he took her papers from her he demanded: "Where is the letter from your husband, saying that he wants your child to go with you?"

For a moment Mum could not speak. Then she managed to say: "Our daughter is only eight years old. It's obvious that my husband wants her to go with me."

But the policeman insisted: "I need a letter from him, otherwise you will have to leave her behind!"

In her panic to get home, (and as she could not afford a taxi), Mum rushed across main roads, narrowly avoiding getting run over by the busy traffic. Irate drivers hooted their horns and shook their fists at her.

She frantically contacted my dad and he cabled the police, giving permission for me to travel to England.

At last it seemed as though there would be no more obstacles, but my mother became increasingly worried about our lack of money. She was worried about not being able to afford to pay for our furniture to be shipped to England. So she rang around various relations to ask for a loan which she said she would repay once our family became settled. All of them were very comfortably off, but said apologetically that they could not help us.

Even my father's mother Francisca, who we knew had quite a lot of money as well as valuable jewellery, told Mum that she could not spare a penny. My mother suggested that my grandmother could sell a couple of pieces of jewellery, but she replied that she wouldn't because it was my inheritance. My mother's last reply to Francisca was that it "would not do Margarete much good if she was in a concentration camp!"

My other grandmother, Tony, wanted to give us all the money she had left, but Mum wouldn't accept that because Tony would need the money to keep herself until she was able to join us.

In desperation, Mum rang our solicitor and he very kindly said he would send us a cheque for 200 marks as a gift and not a loan. In the past the solicitor had earned a lot of money doing my father's business transactions.

Now that the thought of getting out of Germany actually became a reality, I began to feel really sad to leave my grandmother.

Although at the age of eight I remembered my father well, so many things had happened in the six months that he had been away he had become a rather shadowy figure in my mind. I was worried about how I would feel when actually seeing him again.

I also dreaded leaving my old life behind. How would I cope in a strange country where people spoke in a different language? Most of all I wondered how English people would treat us Jews.

Mum and Grandma tried to reassure me that my fears were groundless, but, as a very sensitive eight-year-old child, I could not forget the dreadful things that happened to us.

CHAPTER 5:

GOOD-BYE BERLIN

Just over three years after I had made eye contact with Hitler as he drove through Berlin, my mother and I left Germany in December 1938 to join my father in England.

The evening before we left was full of mixed feelings and emotions. My grandmother and I sat on our sofa. She was diligently knitting, finishing off the coat she had made for my doll so he would be warm on our long journey. My mother was bustling around, labelling our luggage and checking her bag to make sure our papers were all in order.

Aunt Martha and cousin Gunter said their "good-byes" before they went to bed as they would still be asleep when we left early the next morning.

I put my head on Granny Tony's shoulder and thought to myself: "How can I bare to leave her here with all the Nazis?" My eyes began to run with tears and I said to her: "Let me stay with you until your papers come. I don't want to leave you here!"

She answered: "That's lovely of you, darling but it is important that you and Mum go first while I wait for my travel passes to arrive. When you get to England you can telephone me and tell me all about the boarding house where we are going to live. You will also be able to show me around London when I join you."

"But Gran." I pleaded. "How will you manage?"

"I am old enough to look after myself," she replied. "I will keep busy by knitting more clothes for Dolly and thinking of the time when we will all be together again."

Mum then urged me to go to bed because we faced a long journey the next day. Gran stood up and said: "Come on, Deti. I will help you into bed and read you a story."

She sat down beside my bed and her soft voice reading the story was like listening to a lullaby. Even so, my mind was in turmoil, thinking about all the momentous life changing things that were about to happen. I finally dropped off into an uneasy sleep which was full of odd dreams and scary images.

I felt as if I had not slept at all when I awoke on a dark and chilly morning. The day when my mother and I were going to England to join my father had finally arrived. There was a tight knot of anxiety in my stomach, and panic filled the whole of my body at the thought of leaving my old life and particularly my lovely grandmother.

My room was getting lighter now. I looked through my window and saw snow flakes dancing on the pane like graceful ballerinas.

Mum came softly into my room. "It's time to get up now," she said. "The removal men will be here soon." She turned on the light, making me blink at the sudden brightness. "Don't forget to have a good wash!" was her parting shot.

I reluctantly got out of my warm bed and put on the clothes my mother had neatly folded on the chair. I decided not to wash that morning. I felt that it would be a complete waste of time using soap and water as I was bound to get dirty again on our long trip to England. I went over to my dressing table and looked into the mirror without enthusiasm.

I was not a pretty child. My face was too thin,

my black hair was too straight and my teeth were too big for my mouth. Worst of all, because of a pronounced squint in my left eye, I had been forced to wear unbecoming glasses since the age of three. Fortunately, I was usually cheerful and had a lovely big smile which lit up my face, but it was not in evidence that day.

Heaving a sigh, I turned away from the unkind mirror and wished for the umpteenth time that I was beautiful like my mother, or better still, been born a boy. I was convinced that had I been a boy I would have had two straight eyes and been clever and good looking.

The bedroom did not look like mine any more. All the shelves were bare and my toys were in boxes, stacked in a corner. Mum had warned me that all I could take was a few books and my baby doll. I wondered sadly who would be lucky enough to get my toys. I hoped that whoever it was, would look after them.

I went over to the desk that my father had bought for me when I was six and about to start school. I ran my hands lovingly over the smooth wood in a silent goodbye. Finally, I opened the door of my room and promptly fell over a large packing case. One of the removal men yelled: "Don't get in our way, you clumsy Jewish brat!"

Getting up and rubbing my knees, I went into the kitchen. My mother and grandmother were sitting at the table. They looked up when they saw me and smiled; but their smiles were too bright - their eyes were red and I could tell they had been crying.

"Hello, darling," Gran said. "Come and sit down and have your breakfast." I slid onto my chair and for the first time in my life I had no appetite for my

A drawing of my beloved grandmother
Tony, as she looked when I last saw her.

favourite meal of the day, a soft boiled egg and a crusty buttered roll.

I looked at my grandmother. Her white hair was neatly brushed back over her forehead. She had a sweet, round, almost unlined face. Her large brown eyes always looked at me with love. Suddenly the thought of shortly having to leave her filled me with such pain I could hardly breathe. Hot tears poured down my face and through my sobs I managed to gulp: "I can't go to London without you, I want you to come with us now, today."

Gran pulled me on to her lap, took off my glasses and gently wiped my eyes with her snow white hankie that smelled of the scent she always wore. "Look," she said. "I would love to come with both of you today, but you know that my visa has not come yet. As soon as it does I will be on that train and boat like a streak of lighting."

In spite of my misery, I had to smile at the vision of my plump grandmother moving as fast as a streak of lightning. In many ways, she understood me better than either of my parents did.

As my father was building up a lucrative advertising agency it meant he had not been at home a lot and I only saw him at weekends. I knew that my mother loved me, but she had a very active social life and also served on various committees. So I clung to my grandmother. It was into her bed that I crept at night when I had been naughty or had had a bad dream. I told her all my childish secrets and fears. She was always there for me and was always on my side.

One of my most precious memories is of Gran and me sneaking into the kitchen early in the mornings to bake some of her delicious cakes. She let me help her by breaking eggs into a large yellow mixing bowl. If one accidentally fell onto the floor she would laugh, deftly mop it up and say: "Never mind, it's no good crying over broken eggs."

"Now," Gran said firmly. "Sit down and eat your breakfast. You can't go to England on an empty tummy."

"I am not going on my tummy," I laughed. "I am going on a train and a boat!"

Gran pulled a funny face at me and said: "Cheeky!"

I was just finishing my cold egg and roll when one of the removal men came into the kitchen. "We have done all the packing" he informed us.

"Oh, good," said Mum. "Has everything gone on to the van without any trouble?"

"All except a few bits and pieces," he replied curtly.

Mum and I went downstairs with him out into the cold winter morning. To our dismay, we saw my parents' big double bed, with bedding tied onto it, left in the street. But the worst thing of all was that the baby grand piano, (which had belonged to Dad's only sister, a musical prodigy who died long before I was born), was also standing in the road.

"Why are these things not on the van?" Mum asked in alarm.

"I don't know, you stupid Jewish cow!" he snapped. His parting shot before driving off was: "All you Jewish swine are alike. You want something for nothing!"

Mum rang the removal firm's office, but the boss told her that at this late stage there was nothing he could do.

The next few hours passed as though in a dream. Mum checked her bag for our travel papers over and over again. Gran tried to distract me by helping me dress my doll in his outfit that she had knitted for him, but I was still unable to stop the tears running down my face. Then she looked at her watch. "The taxi will be here soon," she said. "It's time to put your coat on."

She helped me into my thick navy blue winter coat. I always hated that coat and longed for a red coat with fur around its collar, but Mum, who dressed in the height of fashion, put me into dark sensible colours. Many years later, my own daughter Francesca would tell me in no uncertain terms what she wanted to wear from the age of five!

Gran tied a scarf around my neck and pulled an ugly woollen hat over my head. It was so itchy that I began to scratch my head underneath it till it slipped down over my forehead and practically landed on my glasses, nearly obscuring my vision. The three of us sat in our hall waiting for the taxi. We did not speak; we just smiled at each other from time to time.

The shrill sound of our bell made us jump. Mum opened the front door to let the driver in, and he took our cases downstairs. We hugged each other briefly. "Go," Gran said. "And do not worry about anything, just get yourselves to England safely." She gently propelled us through the open door.

I held onto Mum's hand as we walked down the stairs and out into the cold, miserable morning. We tried hard not to look at our snow covered furniture standing in the road like abandoned children.

Once in the taxi, I turned to look out of the back window, and saw my grandmother standing on our balcony in order to catch a last glimpse of us. She had not even put her coat on, and the falling snow lay like a white shawl across her shoulders. She looked so lonely standing there, confused and scared in the new and vicious Germany.

I had no way of knowing that this was the last time I would ever see her. My father, who loved her more than he loved his own mother, tried everything he could to get permission for her to join us in England, but it was no use. She was too old, unable to work, and might in time become a burden on the state. It would have been different if my father had been able to assure the authorities that he could afford to support her, but he was earning little money at that time.

Gran died three months after we left her. The doctor diagnosed a heart attack, but I knew that she died because her heart was broken.

A lot of older relatives were left in Germany after

1938. Many did not have the ability or desire to start a new life elsewhere, and those left behind could not go into hiding from the Nazis.

My other grandmother, my father's mother Francisca, thought she was safe in Germany, but this was not the case.

Her oldest son, my uncle Gustav, emigrated to Argentina without saying good-bye to us because he owed my father a lot of money. Instead of getting Grandmother Francisca out of Germany, he arranged for his mother-in-law, who was quite wealthy, to join him in Argentina.

So, at the age of 78, Grandmother Francisca had no family to rely on. She was looked after by her non-Jewish housekeeper Mrs. Gertz until one day when all the flats in her block were searched and the Gestapo found her.

Despite the protests of Mrs. Gertz, who pointed out she was too old and could not do any harm to anybody, the Nazis dragged Francisca out of her flat, threw her into a van and took her into a camp called Theresienstadt where she soon died.

We found all this out from the Red Cross after the war. At the time we had no way of getting news of Grandmother Francisca because any letters that were sent to Jewish relatives were torn up by the Nazis.

CHAPTER 6:

OUR NIGHTMARE JOURNEY

Berlin's railway station was alive with passengers. Business men in bowler hats and smart pin striped suits, carrying brief cases under their arms, were purposefully rushing for their train to begin their daily wheeling and dealing in the metropolis. Others were lining up at the newspaper kiosk, pushing forward, holding out their money to the vendor, anxious not to miss their train.

A group of people with a little girl about my age caught my attention. The child was hugging an elderly lady, obviously her Grandma. They were both crying. I wanted to go over to them and tell the little girl that I understood her grief because I, too, had just said good-bye to my Grandma.

"Don't stare Deti," Mum said. "Come on, we must find our platform for the train. We mustn't miss it. That's it there, it says platform six for Hook of Holland. Come quickly. I think the train is in already."

As we ran down the stairs to platform six, I tripped and fell. I was always falling over something or other. For such a thin child, I was inordinately clumsy.

"Alright?" Mum asked. I nodded and got to my feet. We joined the line of people waiting to have their passports and visas checked. Everyone in the line up looked frightened and nervous. Two men in Nazi uniforms who were standing by the barrier with guns by their side, snatched people's papers out of their hands in order to read them. Their job was to check that everybody crossing the border had the relevant papers and passport.

If any of the travellers did not have the right credentials they would be searched and then sent back.

We seemed to be standing in that line for hours, moving forward at a snail's pace every now and then. I pulled Mum's hand. "I think my knees are bleeding," I said.

Mum told me there was nothing she could do about it until we got on the train. At last it was our turn. One of the men looked at our papers, and shouted at my Mother: "Well, where is it then?"

"Where's what?" Mum asked, confused. "The child's passport, you stupid Jewish whore. I want to see the child's passport."

Mum replied: "But the local police told me that, as my daughter is only eight years old, she could travel on my passport."

"Well, you were told wrong or more than likely you weren't listening," the man barked. "Your daughter can't travel without a passport!"

I began to tremble, thinking that this can't be happening, and that any minute now I would wake up from this frightening nightmare. Mum, with tears in her voice, pleaded with the guard. "I'm sorry, I'm so sorry, that I made such a mistake. I know I should have listened more carefully to the police, it's entirely my fault. I am a stupid woman. Please let me take my daughter with me, I can't leave her here."

The guard turned to his side kick, and they both shook their heads at such gross stupidity. At last he threw our papers on the ground. "Lucky for you, I'm in a good mood today," he said. "Pick up your rubbish, and get out of our Germany, and take your ugly four-eyed brat with you!"

Mum knelt down, trying to retrieve our papers with

shaking hands. I wanted to help, but I felt rooted to the spot, still caught up in this terrible nightmare. I feared that one of the guards might kick my mother with his big boots to make her hurry.

Suddenly a man from a second line of passengers, (who were not emigrating but also going to the Hook of Holland), came over to us and helped my mother to her feet.

He then picked up our papers, handed them to her and helped us onto the train with our luggage. When Mum lowered the window of the carriage and tried to thank him, he put his hand on hers, shook his head and said sadly: "What's our country coming to?"

There were some good Christians in Germany at the time, but they were in the minority. Many of them, who had Jewish people amongst their friends, were appalled at the situation, because Hitler had brain washed the majority, like the youth who had broken my doll. If anyone spoke up in defence of the Jews they would be reported to the Gestapo, running the risk of being imprisoned and possibly killed.

We settled into our compartment. Luckily it was empty, so we were able to leave our cases on the floor. I felt sick, frightened, and very insecure. Mum put her arms around me.

"Are we alright now?" I asked, shakily, "Will they let me go to England with you?"

"Of course they will!" Mum reassured me. "Of course you're coming to England with me."

"Why do people hate us? What have we done that is so bad?" I wanted to know.

Mum thought for a moment and told me: "Hitler, the new leader of Germany, is a very strange man, and for some reason he does not like Jewish people.

He has told a lot of German people that we Jews are greedy, and not very nice."

"Will the English people hate us, too?" I asked.

"Oh, no," Mum replied. "They like us very much."

"How do you know that?" I persisted.

"Because Dad has written many letters, telling me how kind English people have been to him. The ladies, who own the boarding house where we are going, are lovely people and have other Jewish families from Germany staying there."

I relaxed a little and shut my eyes. The movement of the train made me drowsy, and I dropped off to sleep. Suddenly the train screeched to a grinding halt and a loud voice shouted, "Bentheim, border of Bentheim, have travel papers ready."

I looked at Mum and I could see could see that she was frightened. She told me much later that Bentheim was the border that everyone dreaded because if the guards did not like the look of anyone, they would arrest them on any pretext. These people were never seen or heard of again.

Some foolhardy people who tried to smuggle jewellery or money out of Germany, either in their clothing or by swallowing it, were stripped and beaten, sometimes to death.

Well-meaning friends in Berlin had suggested to Mum that she could smuggle some of my paternal grandmother's valuable jewellery somewhere on her person, but she had wisely refused to do so.

All my mother and grandmother wanted was for us to get safely out of Germany, which meant leaving everything of value of behind. All our possessions could be replaced but our lives could not.

There was much slamming of carriage doors, and men's voices shouting. The door of our carriage was flung open and a tall young Nazi officer came in. He looked at Mum with interest, because despite her pallor and deep shadows under her eyes, she still managed to look beautiful.

"Anything to declare?" he asked pleasantly.

Mum shook her head. "No, nothing," she replied.

"Good," he said and chalked our cases with a large white cross. Encouraged by his friendly manner, I caught hold of his sleeve and asked in my politest voice: "Please I've some pfennigs in my pocket, may I take them to England?"

The man patted me on the head and said: "Sure you can," and, turning to Mum, he added: "Nice little girl." Then, with a half-hearted "Heil Hitler", he stepped out of our carriage and out of our lives.

I wondered why my mother had looked so terribly frightened. I sensed her fear which sent cold shivers down my back, and I began to tremble.

I thought we may have done something wrong. But then I witnessed something terrible which made me frightened, too.

As the train pulled slowly away from the station, we looked out of the window and saw a man laying on the ground, being repeatedly kicked and spat on by Nazi guards. Next to him a woman was holding onto two small children who were screaming. Their luggage was strewn on the ground around them, with clothes, toys and other belongings.

Mum pulled me away from the window and drew the small curtain across it. We sat for a long time holding onto each other, trying hard not to think of this family and the terrible things that may be happening to them.

I don't know the reason why this young family were so persecuted. The guards probably didn't like to see a young Jewish family leaving Germany and trying to start a new life elsewhere. Or maybe they just didn't like the look of them. I fear the man was probably killed by the guards, and the woman and her children sent to a concentration camp.

When we were safe in England I asked my mother why she had had been so frightened even before we had seen the man being beaten up. She told me that if the German guards did not like the look of someone they were prone to pull them from the train. Or if they fancied some women, and wanted them for their own purposes, they were also known to take them off the train, leaving their screaming children behind.

A book by Thomas Craughwell called 'Great Rescues of World War II' tells how the children in the 'Kinder transport rescue mission' were terrified by the brutal Nazi regime when passing through this border in 1938.

This book recalls that a group of 196 Jewish orphans, whose orphanage had been burnt down by the Nazis, were the first group of children to use the kinder transport. When they got to the Dutch-German border the SS boarded the train and ransacked all the children's luggage, looking for illegal items. They behaved like animals, breaking open the suitcases and damaging items, including the children's toys in the process.

The children were terrified. When the organisers of the transport saw what was happening they had some stern words with the Nazis, who finally stopped. The children were then able to board another train bound for the ferry. They caught it, then disembarked in England at Harwich on December 2nd, 1938.

Aunt Martha's nephew by marriage, Stephen Somerfield, sadly had to leave his parents behind and was put on the kinder transport. Luckily, his journey to England went off without any trouble, but unfortunately the elderly couple he was fostered with were not terribly kind and did not show much interest in him.

When he was 16 they made him become an apprentice to a gardener. But Stephen was more ambitious than this. So he took a teacher's training course, secured a job as a form master and worked his way up to becoming a deputy head of a big grammar school.

He later met and married a charming woman called Eugene. They had a little boy called James and, a couple of years later, twin girls.

My mother and I were on the train for three days. I went through a mixture of emotions: boredom, frustration and sadness at having to leave my grandmother. There was also horror and fear when I closed my eyes and remembered the man who Mum and I saw being tortured on the platform at Bentheim. I sometimes heard the children's desperate screams when I woke in the night, bathed in sweat and filled with terror. I wished with all my heart that my grandmother was with us so that I could creep into her bed and hear her say softly "It's all right darling, it's alright."

I was scared of our new life in England. I wondered how quickly I would be able to learn the new language and if I would make friends with the English children. I was also nervous about meeting my father again, even though at the age of eight I remembered him well. So much had happened in the six months he had been away from us that he had become a rather shadowy figure in my life.

The only bright spot during our long and tedious journey was the breakfast and dinner we had in the dining car on the first day. Mum explained to me that we could only choose food from the set menu and not à la carte, where you have more choices, but pay more for them.

The food on the set menu was quite good, but because I was a very finicky eater, I did not like anything other than the breakfasts. I loved to watch the other diners and stared at them with great interest despite Mum's strict instructions not to do so.

I was just a born starer. For example, when Mum and I had been in the lovely Tiergarten Park in Berlin, I caught sight of a dwarf. "Look Mum," I shouted excitedly, "Look at that tiny man, he seems quite old, but he's much smaller than me."

"Come here," Mum urged, but undeterred, I ran in front of him and asked: "Why is he so small?" I don't know who was more embarrassed, the poor man or Mum.

When we got back home, Mum gave me a strict lecture that I must never again make remarks about a person's personal appearance.

But when my grandmother and I used to go out together we made up stories about people we saw at tram stops, or in the café we often visited.

Now, during our long train journey, I longed for my grandmother with all my heart. I wanted to talk to her and tell her how confused and sad I was.

Mum allowed me to walk up and down the corridor for a short while in order to stretch my restless legs. I looked intently into each compartment as I passed on my way. A young couple with a pretty baby smiled at me. I stood watching as the mother gave her baby it's bottle. In the next compartment, an elderly couple were asleep. I could hear them snoring very loudly. I wondered why their snores did not wake them up.

I then came across one couple with their arms around each other and their mouths pressed together. I could not understand how it was possible for them to breathe in this position and waited, fascinated, to see if they would choke to death. At last they separated. The man looked up and saw me standing there with my nose pressed tightly against the window. He got up, shook his fist and pulled the small curtain across the pane. Mum put her head out of the door of our compartment. "Deti," she called, crossly, "Come back now and do some drawing!"

At last we arrived at The Hook of Holland. It felt strange walking on solid ground again. I quite missed the swaying movements of the train. I started feeling safer as the worse part of the journey was over.

Mum told me to sit on a bench for a minute, and began to rummage in her bulky handbag. After a few moments she brought out the dreaded hat. "Here, darling," she said, "Put this on, it's very cold and very windy." I took it from her, looking at it with distaste.

She then walked a little way along the platform to look for the sign to the wharf. This was my chance. While she was walking with her back towards me, I got off the bench, walked a little nearer to the edge of the platform, lifted my arm and threw the hat as hard as I could onto the railway lines. To my great joy a train came slowly into the station and reduced my hat to a mangled mass of knitwear.

"Mum," I cried, in consternation, "I've lost my hat. It blew onto the track and is ruined now." She came back to the seat where I was sitting with a sad expression on my face. "How could it blow away?" she asked in a puzzled voice. "Did you do it on purpose?"

I tried to make my eyes behind my glasses look

hurt and innocent at such a suggestion. "Of course not," I assured her. I was a very convincing liar. It was only a white lie, I comforted myself. "A white lie is no different from a black one," Mum always told me whenever she caught me out.

A man in uniform suddenly appeared. I began to tremble and feel scared again, but he had no swastika on his arm and no gun by his side. Instead, he asked in a friendly voice, "Can I help you ladies?" That pleased me enormously. I had never been called a lady before.

"We're looking for the wharf," Mum told him. "Come with me, I'll lead the way," the man replied. He put our cases onto a trolley, and we followed him. The boat was already in dock.

"Here you are, ladies," the porter told us. "Join the line over there for passport checks, and then go aboard." Mum thanked him for his trouble and gave him a shilling. He touched his cap and walked back to the station.

I began to feel nervous at the thought of having our passport checked again. But a man dressed in a naval uniform smiled at us and said: "Welcome aboard. I hope you'll have a pleasant voyage."

We were taken by a young steward to our cabin, which was third class and very small. There was just enough room for a double bunk, a small cupboard and a hand basin. Mum found another shilling and gave it to the steward. "Now," she told me urgently, "Ask him now!" This was my moment of glory. I looked up at the young man and said the only English sentence I knew, taught to me by English-speaking friends in Berlin. "Please will you wake us one hour before the steamer stops?"

We were too tired to go into the dinning room for supper. I climbed up into the top bunk and Mum slid into the lower one. The soft lulling of the boat sent me to sleep almost straight away, but I don't think that Mum slept at all because she looked as tired the next morning as she had done on the night before.

The boat landed in Harwich early and we made our way to the station to get the train to Liverpool Street where Dad would be waiting for us. It was bitterly cold, the wind made my ears sting, and for a fleeting moment I wished that I had not thrown the dreaded woollen hat onto the railway track.

We settled in the train, on the last lap of our journey. Just as the train was about to leave, a man panted into our compartment. He said, "Good morning" and smiled, showing black and broken teeth. He sat down next to Mum and, taking a crumpled paper bag out of his pocket, offered us a sweet. We politely said, "No thanks."

He then spoke non-stop to Mum who kept replying "Yes." He pushed up against her, until she was squashed against the window. Luckily he got out at the next stop and, with a courtly bow, handed Mum his card as he departed. I often wondered what it was she said "yes" to.

We arrived at our destination and struggled to get out of the train. We immediately became engulfed in a thick grey and evil smelling smoke. I held onto Mum's hand for dear life.

The smoke was so dense that we literally could not see our hands before our faces. I opened my mouth and shouted to Mum, "The station is on fire. We will be burned to death!" My throat filled with the polluted air, making me feel as if I was choking.

I remember thinking: 'How in all this terrible smoke will we ever find my father?' In my vivid imagination

I could see Mum and me walking around and around this station for ever.

Other people who were also trying to find their way out of the station were continually bumping into each other. We trudged blindly, having no idea where we were going, when suddenly, like a miracle, a familiar voice called out of the gloom. "Selli, Deti, is that you?"

"Yes!" I shouted, "It's us, it's really us."

I ran towards this voice and in the next moment was swept up into my father's arms. I rubbed my face against his. It felt rough, as though he had not had the time for a shave that morning. Now he was no longer a shadowy figure, but my dear dependable Dad who never let me down. Mum came up to us, put down our cases, and threw her arms around him. The three of us clung together, with tears of joy and relief running down our faces.

When we had composed ourselves a little, Dad said, "Now we must go down to the underground and get the train to Bayswater, and then a taxi to the boarding house."

"Oh no," I moaned, "Not another train, not another one. We've been on hundreds of trains - I'm thirsty and my feet hurt."

"This is the last train you'll have to go on," Dad said. "Mum told me how grown up you've been - just be patient for a little while longer."

We went down loads of steps into the bowels of the earth. The underground was packed with people, all pushing and shoving to get to the edge of the platform. A train thundered into the station, and it's red doors slid open.

Mum and I were literally propelled onto to it and, to my dismay, I could not see Dad. "Papi," I cried in alarm, "Papi, where are you? Oh, Mum we've lost him again. What shall we do?"

The other passengers gazed at me with sympathy. Some of them bent down to look under the seats because they believed 'papi' meant dog. I remember thinking 'Strange people, these English. How could Dad possibly be hiding under the narrow seats?' Just then, Dad managed to push his way over to us. I nearly fainted with relief!

The next stop was ours. Loads of other people also got out and we were able to alight without any mishaps. Dad hailed a taxi, and Mum and I sank into the back seats. The smoke had completely gone now, and I looked with interest at the London streets. "Where's the smoke gone?" I asked, "That wasn't smoke, Dad replied, "That was fog - the English call it the good old pea soup."

"And why?" I went on, "Did some people look under the seats when we lost you on the train?"

He explained that they thought I was looking for my dog – and the English love dogs.

"So do I. Can I have a dog?" I implored.

"Not while we live here," Dad said. "Can you imagine what it would be like if all the guests in the boarding house had a dog. It would be a dog house."

For a moment I imagined the delight of living in a house full of dogs, all running around, wagging their tails.

CHAPTER 7:

OUR TORMENT

The taxi took us to a square sort of street, with a patch of grass in the middle of it, surrounded by trees.

Dad was just about to put his key into a green front door when it was opened by a smiling middle-aged lady in a black dress, with white lace around the collar and cuffs. This reminded me of the dresses Gran always wore, and I began to miss her all over again.

"This is Miss Mavis," Dad announced. Miss Mavis kissed both Mum and me and said, "Hello." Her kiss was a bit wet, but I did not wipe my face in case she thought that I was rude.

Dad spoke to her in what I thought then was perfect English and, still smiling broadly, she went down a flight of stairs, disappearing from view. Dad then opened the door and took us into the room which was to be our home for the unforeseeable future.

It was of medium size, sparsely furnished, with two arm chairs, a table and three small chairs, a wardrobe and a chest of drawers. There was a single bed along one wall and a double bed along the other.

Mum sank onto the double bed and burst into tears of exhaustion and sadness. Dad sat down beside her and put a comforting arm around her shoulders. The room felt cold, and when Dad saw me give a little shiver, he got up to put a match to a strange contraption against one of the walls. This odd looking thing hissed and spluttered. Then it glowed, and gradually our room became a little warmer.

Mum went out into the hall and put some money into a large pay phone to ring Gran. When she had finished speaking, she let me talk to her. Gran said she was fine, but, knowing her voice as well as I did, I knew she was only saying that to stop me from worrying. In reality she was very sad. My eyes filled with tears as I said goodbye to her, but I blinked them away before I went back into our room so as not to upset Mum.

We were thankful to be safe in England, but we were were still racked with worry and torment about what was likely to happen to our fellow Jews at the hands of the Nazis in Germany. Stories and rumours were rife about what was going on back home.

It was against this background that we began our new lives in Bayswater. The ladies who owned the boarding house, Miss Mavis and Miss Maud, were kind and well meaning. They had inherited the house from their parents, whom they had looked after until their death.

Miss Mavis and Miss Maud took in refugee families at a very cheap rent. Unfortunately they were not business people, and ran the house at a loss because they did not charge the other lodgers enough. They were also much too easy on their staff, who did the minimum amount of work, and the bad tempered cook ruined the food the ladies ordered.

The first morning we went into the dinning room for breakfast we were shown to a corner table by a harassed-looking waitress. Dad asked her for coffee, toast and jam, and a softly boiled egg for me.

While waiting for our breakfast to arrive, I looked at our fellow lodgers with my usual interested stare. There were six tables in the room, mostly occupied by men who ate their food quickly and then left for work. Two middle-aged ladies caught my attention. I looked at them as they carefully broke their toast into squares, buttering each piece with great concentration and chewing each bit about 100 times. I was sure that they would still be chewing away till dinner time.

At last our waitress, looking more harassed than before, hurried over to us, carrying our breakfast on a tray. Mum poured the coffee, which looked like brown water, and when I cut the top off my egg its contents ran on to my plate. It looked as though it had not been boiled at all! So I had to make do with hard dry toast and butter.

Just as we were about to leave the dinning room, a family came in. Dad introduced us to Mrs. Brown and her husband, a teacher, who had come over from Austria four months ago with their son, daughter and beautiful baby. The girl's name was Susan and she became my new friend.

Susan and I soon became the terrors of the boarding house. We would burst into the kitchen, ignore the shouts of the red-faced, greasy-looking cook to get out, and run around the kitchen table, helping ourselves to any cakes or biscuits laying there.

Our next mission was to race up the backstairs and knock over the bucket of soapy water with which the cleaner was halfheartedly washing the floor. Our favourite activity, however, was answering the telephone. As soon as it rang, we were there, taking turns to answer it. "Hello," we would say, "what do you want?" When the caller told us, we would reply "Wait a mina (minute)," and run off, leaving the receiver dangling in mid-air and the poor caller waiting at the other end!

Looking back, it seems quite incredible to me how quickly I settled into my new life. Much to my parents' and my own astonishment, I soaked up the English language like a sponge and at the end of three weeks I spoke it almost fluently.

My parents, however, found the new language hard to learn, and I was ashamed by their strong accent. So whenever we went shopping I refused to let them open their mouths and I asked the shopkeeper for whatever we wanted.

My mother was very unhappy. She missed my Grandma and hated her new life. She just did not know what to do with herself during her long and boring day. She had always been in charge, busily running her home, but now she had nothing to do.

Dad also had his problems. He hated his job as a toy rep, travelling around London all day trying to sell a garish sailor doll with red painted face. When you wound up the doll by a large key, at the back, it sang 'God save the king'.

My parents were also distressed about the news that Jewish people were suffering at the hands of the Nazis. But although I still worried about my grandmother, I was so taken up with my friend Susan and the new people I was meeting that my life in Berlin seemed far away.

When Mrs. Brown saw how much I loved babies, she let me help her to bathe her baby and feed him. Sitting on the chair, holding him in my arms while he drank milk, was heaven for me.

Ever since I could remember I had longed for a baby brother or sister. I asked Mum while still in Berlin why we could not have one. She told me that in order to get a baby, people had to put salt on their window sill and if they were lucky a stork would leave a baby there. Even though I was scared of the dark, I used to creep out of bed in the middle of the night, wrench open the heavy kitchen window and sprinkle some salt on to the sill. I remember hoping that the baby would not fall off the narrow window sill, but comforted myself with the thought that if the stork was clever enough to find us a baby, he would surely find a way of not letting the baby fall.

Every night for a week I repeated the salt-sprinkling ritual. Mum got more and more irritated at finding salt trailing across the floor every morning. She even blamed our housekeeper Greta for not sweeping the floor in the evenings. Greta was offended at this accusation, and spent the rest of the day sulking in her room. So I sadly decided to give up my nightly quest, thinking that the reason the stork had not left us a baby was that I must have been using the wrong type of salt.

All good things come to an end. In February, Mr. Brown got a regular teaching job, so he and his family moved into a flat near the school which, unfortunately, was at the other side of town.

Susan and I said a tearful goodbye and swore that we would be friends forever, but when we went to see the family in their new home, I found that she and I had grown apart. She was caught up in her new life and talked endlessly about the friends she had made in her new school.

I was left feeling very sad and lonely. My parents then decided that I, too, should go to school.

CHAPTER 8:

BAY'S SCHOOL

Despite my protests, I found myself one Monday morning, holding tight to my parents' hands outside a school. It looked more like a church in disrepair than a school, with a steeple leaning to one side, so I said to my father: "This can't be a school. It looks like a church."

"No," he assured me. "It is a school. Look, it says 'Bay's Junior and Infant school. Head Mrs. Thompson'."

We pushed open the heavy door and I found myself in a children's paradise. It was a big hall, full of bright mats on the floor. The walls were decorated with pictures, which I reckoned were what the pupils had painted.

Children sat in corners of the room, doing different things. There was an aura of peace about it, so different to my school in Berlin, where there was shouting, running around and not much discipline. In one corner there were little girls, sitting in what looked like a tent. I later found out it was a Wendy house. They were busy washing and dressing dolls. In another corner some children were reading and some drawing, standing by an easel. Others were dressed in long aprons, sloshing paint around.

There was also a shop, with a line of children waiting patiently to give two 'shopkeepers' their toy money in exchange for one or two boxes. I had never seen anything like that before. I thought it was amazing.

A nice young lady came across to us. "Hello" she said. "Are you Mr. and Mrs. Mendelsohn and Margarete?"

When my father confirmed that we were, I thought 'I hope his English won't be too bad'.

The lady took us to meet the headmistress Mrs. Thompson, who asked if I spoke any English. "Oh, yes" my father replied, in his thick German accent. "She speaks almost perfect English. In fact she won't even speak to us!"

Mrs. Thompson turned to me and said: "I've got a good idea, Margarete. As this is your first day, would you like to stay with us for the morning and just see how you like it, and your mum and dad can pick you up lunchtime?"

I suddenly got a bit scared, but then I thought about that lovely hall and all the things in it. So I said "Yes please!" My parents now looked more frightened than me as they left!

Mrs. Thompson took me to a classroom where she introduced me to the teacher, Miss Gates, and the pupils. She said: "This is Margarete. It's her first time in this school. She has come a long way to be with us, from Berlin in Germany. But she speaks quite good English already. I want you to make her welcome." Then she left to return to her office.

Miss Gates sat me next to a girl called Cynthia and asked her to look after me. Cynthia did not look terribly happy at this prospect; and was busy biting her nails. "Don't do that," said Miss Gates, while taking Cynthia's hand out of her mouth. No sooner had she done this than Cynthia began on her other hand.

We opened reading books and to my delight I found I could understand some of the simple sentences. The children stood up in turn to read out loud. Some of them read well, some didn't.

"Margarete, how are you getting on?" inquired the teacher. "Could you read us a few words?"

"Yes please," I said shyly and stood up.

"Jill and Jack stood on the mat, then Jill took the k-nife," and everyone laughed. "Stop laughing children," Miss Gates said. "Margarete, we have a very funny language. We have what we call silent letters. Although it says K N I F E, we pronounce it (K)nife. There are lots of words like that. I am sure you will soon learn them."

Soon after I had finished reading a bell sounded. "Playtime," Miss Gates announced. "Come along, children, take Margarete out and show her what to do."

As it was winter and very cold, we had our playtime in the hall. The children formed a ring around me. They were very friendly. One girl asked me: "Are you really from Germany?"

"Yes," I said.

"Say something in German" she urged me.

"No, I would really rather not," I said.

"Go on!" she insisted.

All the children looked at me expectantly so I said: "Wie Giltest dir."

"What does that mean?" she asked.

I told her that it meant 'how are you?'

"Well, I never did!" she replied.

Some of the children were very badly dressed. And several of the girls looked at me in envy because my mother let me wear my best clothes to school. I hadn't many left as I had grown so much. So I wore a navy blue skirt, a white shirt and a white cardigan, with white socks and black shoes.

Suddenly Miss Gates came out, carrying a small tray with lots of bottles of milk on it. She handed each of us a bottle. I didn't like milk much, but when I tried it with a straw it tasted surprisingly good. I slurped happily with the other children.

Another bell sounded. "Break's over," announced Miss Gates. We all filed back into the classroom.

In the next half hour Miss Gates read us a story about a little girl called Alice, who fell down a big hole and found herself in a wonderland where she had tea with the mad hatter. I didn't know what a hatter was, but I thought it must be really good. When she finished the story she said: "Come along children, dinner time!"

I saw my parents standing at the door. Miss Gates took me to meet them. "Did you enjoy it?" she asked me.

"Oh yes, I did!" I replied.

Miss Gates said: "We shall finish the story tomorrow!"

She got me my coat as my new friends looked on. "Goodbye! See you tomorrow." "Yes," I said happily, "See you tomorrow!"

As we walked back, my mother asked: "Well, how did you like it?"

So I answered with the same phrase my children would always answer to me in later years. I sighed and said: "It was alright."

The three months I spent in that little run-down junior school in the slums of Bayswater were the happiest and most positive of all my school days. The dedicated teachers let each child work at their own pace. No one criticised, only encouraged. I occasionally got a pinch from another child in the playground because they seemed to be jealous that the teacher regularly asked me to read out my essays, but everyone was good humoured and friendly.

So I looked forward to going to school every day, whereas in Berlin I had dreaded school, mainly because I was put in the back of the class and, as I was short sighted, I could not see the board.

I made friends with a girl at my new school called Beryl, who lived across the road from us. She was a couple of years older than me and offered to walk me home, which my mother reluctantly agreed to, following a lot of pleading by me. Every day I waited for Beryl outside the school because she finished a little bit later than me.

One day Beryl didn't turn up. I could have gone into the school and asked my teacher for help, but I decided to go home on my own.

Unfortunately, I took a wrong turning. I had no sense of direction. I still haven't. I seemed to walk for miles and miles, passing lamp posts. There were no landmarks. I started getting panicky; wondering what I should do. There was no way of contacting my mother and she would be going berserk, not knowing were I was.

Suddenly I walked into two long legs, dressed in navy blue.

"What's wrong little girl?" I looked up into the face of a great big policeman.

"I am lost," I said.

"Where do you live, darling?" he asked.

I told him, amid sobs, that I lived in a boarding house in Porchester Square.

"Don't cry, dry your eyes," he said. He gave me a great big hanky, which I blew into. I gave it back to him, but he was not that happy to take it!

He took me to Porchester Square where we found my poor mother shouting and crying and screaming in the road.

The lovely policeman, whose name was Tom, came in with us for a cup of tea and became a firm friend.

He used to call in from time to time when he was passing on his beat. What a shame that nowadays you don't find policeman on the street. It would prevent so many terrible things that happen to adults and children. If I had not had met Tom, I do not know what I would have done.

Anyway, that put an end to my independence. From then on my mother took me to school and fetched me. We practically ignored Beryl, whose non-appearance that day was never fully explained to me.

Then we received the very bad news that my lovely grandmother Antonia had passed away. As a child I thought she had died of a broken heart, but it was probably due to loneliness and the fear of what might happen to her if she were arrested.

My mother was devastated, desolate, at losing her mother, and so was I. My dad was also extremely upset. Another reason for his unhappiness was that he hated his job, travelling around London trying to sell toys, so there was a terrible atmosphere in our little room in the boarding house.

Things got worse, with my mother becoming depressed, and I used to pour out my heart to my sympathetic teacher Miss Gates.

I don't think my parents could see any way out of the mess we were in. Then my father had a stroke of good luck. When he stopped for a cup of tea in one of the Lyon's corner tea houses, he bumped into an old acquaintance, Mr. Haulfarmer, who he knew vaguely in Berlin.

Mr. Haulfarmer and his wife had come to England four years before us. He was building up a fairly lucrative advertising agency and offered my dad a job on a three month trial in his firm. He also told Dad about a flat that was available in an area called

Wembley. There was a generous landlord and the rent would be 32 shillings and six pence a week, which I think in today's money would be around one pound and fifty pence.

My parents and I went to see the flat. It was set in a very nice court, but the flat itself badly needed decorating and we couldn't afford to do it. There was a long hall with a kitchen to the right. Then there was a small bedroom leading onto a balcony. This was going to be my room. The lounge was a medium size and then there was another small hall which led onto a bathroom, toilet and another bedroom.

I said a very sad goodbye at school to my friends and my teachers.

We moved into Empire Court, Wembley, in February, 1939. Funnily enough, when we got to Wembley my mother and I reversed roles. She was more cheerful as she could clean, cook and go shopping. In contrast, I became very sad because I kept thinking about how my grandmother would have liked it. I spent many nights in bed, crying my eyes out.

The block of flats contained some interesting people. There was a lady upstairs, Mrs. Baron, who was like the matriarch of the refugees. She held 'court' in her flat once a week, with lovely Viennese pastries. I remember feeling sorry for her son, a downtrodden man who was married to a very bossy wife.

On the next floor was a rather jolly English lady called Aida Rowe. She had long, grey hair and wore lots of bangles, and she liked to go out walking with a young man. My mother told me: "Look! What a wonderfully devoted mother and son."

Aida knocked on our door one day and said: "Welcome to our little conclave here." She invited me to have tea with herself and her husband in their flat.

Obviously, the young man we thought was her son was actually her husband!

The next week I duly went up to their flat and took Mrs. Rowe a bunch of flowers. She was very friendly, and I soon found myself telling her how our life had been in Germany. When she heard about my doll being chucked onto the road she was very sympathetic and gave me a big hug.

She informed me that she had a niece of my age called Jean, who was recovering from injury after falling out of the front passenger seat of her dad's car a few months earlier.

When her husband Don arrived home, Mrs. Rowe rushed up to him, put her hands round his neck and kissed him. She then served us both a wonderful meal of mashed potatoes, sausages and some little red things which swam in a tomato sauce. I later learned that they were called baked beans. This was followed by trifle. I had not had such a great meal since moving to England. It was delicious!

From that day onwards, mash, sausages, beans and trifle has been one of my favourite meals.

As I was growing so fast and my parents could ill afford to buy me any new clothes, my father went to a community centre for Jewish people called Bloomsbury House where the wealthy donated clothes for refugees. When he came back home with clothes in his bag my first reaction was: "I would rather wear my normal clothes than those!"

Among the clothes for me was a tweedy coat, which was thread bare at the elbows, and a pork pie hat. There were also two or three much worn dresses.

When we went to the synagogue we were accompanied by a girl called Catherine Bird, who we nicknamed 'The Peacock' because she was always dressed in the height of fashion. I, in my brown tweedy coat, pork pie hat and cuffed shoes, walked behind her like a pauper.

CHAPTER 9:

LIFE GETS WORSE

Life changed for the worse from the time my Aunt Martha and cousin Gunter came over from Germany to join us in our flat about a month after we moved in.

In order to ensure their emigration to England my father had to find a guarantor who would put up a required sum of money. He found an extremely nice lady who was very pro Jewish. This enabled my aunt and cousin to come and live with us, which made life more difficult as, at times, we did not get on well together!

My cousin was still terribly spoilt and my aunt ran after him like a slave. He had a bit of respect for my father, but not much.

The same scenario developed that we had in Berlin, with me not being allowed to go out with my friends. Gunter was to blame for this. He was a demanding boy who didn't like me playing with the English friends I had made. Whenever anyone called for me Gunter told his mother that he felt another epileptic fit was coming on.

It caused a lot of friction, and to make matters worse Gunter would hide my books so that I could not even read at home. This bought back a lot of the feelings of trauma I had experienced during the last few months in Berlin and I was very unhappy.

It had been stressful for Grandmother Tony when she lived with Gunter and his mother in Germany, and apparently she had looked tired and worn out before dying from a heart attack. Thinking about her made me cry.

I was now getting thoroughly fed up, especially as I had been so happy when we first came to England. My mother and my aunt started falling out. Money was very tight, so Aunt Martha and Mum bought food separately. However, my mother found that Aunt Martha had taken a piece of chicken from our pot and put it into hers. My father was really getting upset with the situation and there was a terrible atmosphere.

It seemed that things could not get much worse – but they did! At the worst possible time, in the Spring of 1939, my father lost his job.

His boss, Mr. Haulfarmer told him that he didn't think my father was cut out for advertising in this country because he had got a different mentality. The upshot was that he was not going to renew dad's contract.

My poor father was unemployed again and didn't know what to do. He briefly got a job in a factory, which he disliked intensely.

Meanwhile, my aunt decided to do a bit of cleaning and found work with a few Jewish people. But she still could not afford to buy beds for herself and my cousin. They were sleeping on a mattress in the main bedroom, while my parents slept in the lounge on a double put-you-up.

My father decided to build two beds and bought some Hessian and wooden beams. Unfortunately, he was no handy man! We could hear him swearing and cursing all evening when he hit his thumb with a hammer.

The people downstairs began to bang on the ceiling. So my mother went downstairs and said, (in broken English): "I am sorry about the noise, but my husband is trying to make two beds for my sister and her son." The man was very nice and offered to help make the beds, which he did.

Aunt Martha and cousin Gunter now had a bed to sleep on. My father was so grateful to the neighbour who had helped build them that he gave him some chocolates.

My parents enrolled me in the local 'Wembley Hill Junior and Senior school'. It was nowhere near as good as my previous school in Bayswater. Here I was a small fish in a large pond. I was rubbish at everything, apart from English, but nobody gave me any praise for my excellent dictation and spelling.

I hated the school. All the children teased me and called me 'black death' and 'boss eyed' or 'four eyes, on account of my glasses.

Things did get slightly better for me when a family called Jones moved into our block in the upstairs flat and I became friends with their lovely daughter Marion.

She was taller than me and very pretty, with beautiful brunette hair which fell into a natural pageboy across her shoulders. We used to walk to school together because she was in my class. I used to imagine how it would feel if I had a lovely page boy hair style, swinging from side to side as I walked along!

Marion was brighter than me. She was better at maths and other subjects, with the exception of English. We used to spend a lot of time together. We both liked the 'Just Williams' books by Richmal Crompton and when we saw the latest edition being sold in the shops we would go halves to buy them. We pretended that we had a brother called William and talked about all the naughty things he did!

During the summer holidays we had a great time. We would go for picnic lunches to a place I knew as Kitchendom. It was full of factories and there was a filthy stream, but we would sit by an equally dirty pond, fishing for tadpoles, reading our books and talking about William. We really enjoyed ourselves. In those days there were no problems for children going out to play on the own.

One of the neighbours, who had been a teacher in her native country, tried to teach the older people, many of them German and Austrian Jewish refugees, to speak proper English.

There were quite a few middle aged and elderly couples in the flats. They were able to come to England from Germany because they were quite comfortably off and would not become a burden on the state. Unfortunately, my two grandmothers had been prevented from joining us because my father had earned so little money at the time that he could not guarantee to the government that he was able to support them.

CHAPTER 10:

THE SLAUGHTER OF THE JEWS

In the early summer of 1939 there was a lot of speculation that there may be a second world war.

Britain's then prime minister Neville Chamberlain, famous for his umbrella, had a meeting with Adolf Hitler and got an assurance that he would not invade Poland. But it proved to be meaningless. A few weeks later Germany invaded Poland, and Chamberlain made a speech on the radio saying that we were at war with Germany.

Although my parents and I felt much safer in England, we continued to be haunted by fears that the Nazis were ill treating our relatives and friends who were unable to get out of Germany in time.

We found out that as the Nazi control spread throughout Europe there were more and more deportations of Jewish people. From 1939 until 1941 this happened in Austria, Hungary and France. There were also ghettos in Poland where Jewish people were sectioned off by walls. Conditions in the ghettos were terrible and many died of various diseases.

Later the Nazis started to developed the 'Final Solution' where they sent Jews to their death. In all there were about 100 concentration camps all over Europe.

Ironically, some of my school mates were completely unaware of how much we Jews were suffering, and actually believed I was a German informant!

At school one morning a group of children danced round me singing "German spy! German spy!"

Our teacher Mr. Angel found me crying in the

playground and said to my classmates: "This girl Margarete has more reason to hate the Germans than you do. She and her parents were nearly arrested by the Germans and had to escape to England, leaving everything behind, including Margarete's grandmother, who died shortly after they left.

"If I hear one more word from any of you, taunting Margarete for being a Jewish German refugee, I can assure you that there will be a lot of trouble in store for you."

This distressing episode in my life included my father being forced to leave our home because all men from Germany who were living in Britain had to be interned for the duration of the war.

Dad and fellow refugees outside internment camp, Isle of Man 1939. Alfred fourth from right.

First, they all had to attend a tribunal where a panel decided who was most suspicious and gave them categories. My father was in the least suspicious group, but was told, nevertheless, that he was going to be confined.

On a morning in November, 1939 a lorry arrived to pick up all the German men and take them to Douglas in the Isle of Man. A couple of elderly women ran into the street, crying and waving their hands in the air with despair. My mother went over to them and said crossly: "Stop this at once! Thank God that your husbands are not going to a concentration camp in Germany. They are only going to an intern camp in England!"

All the interned men aged between 20 and 50 were given the option of joining the 'Pioneer Corp' which my father did, knowing that it would enable him to come home on leave every three months. Due to the fact he had fallen arches, as a result of suffering from Scarlet Fever, he was assigned to the kitchen where constantly peeling potatoes caused his hands to blister.

The upside was that he got plenty to eat and when he visited us every three months from his base in Devon he brought with him a 'goodie bag' of food, which lifted our spirits during this period of rationing.

My dear father Alfred was discharged on medical grounds after two years because his problems with his feet prevented him taking part in parades.

Ironically, poor health had also prevented Alfred serving long in the German army during the First World War. After a year he had become so desperately ill with dysentery that he was discharged.

Following his spell in the pioneer core, he got a job in an ammunitions factory near Wembley and worked there until the end of the war. His return was a double cause for celebration because it led to my bossy cousin Gunter and his mother moving into a bed sit, and our life returning to normal.

CHAPTER 11:

FORCED TO COMMIT SUICIDE

Many of our fellow refugees had been in great danger of going to the concentration camps, but had managed to get out of Germany in the nick of time. Tragically, some of those left behind decided to kill themselves and their children rather than be sent to these prison hell holes.

My father's uncles, aunts and young cousins had contributed so much towards the German economy, yet they were now faced with being thrown into these terrible camps. Consequently, they decided to poison their children and then themselves.

They were driven to commit suicide because it was the lesser of two awful evils.

Conditions in the concentration camps were appalling. Thousands of prisoners died of starvation, disease, exhaustion through over work, exposure to the elements, or being executed for alleged crimes.

Then, in early 1942, the Nazis' 'Final Solution' saw them equip camps for the express purpose of mass extermination, principally of Jews, but of other groups as well. This was by means of gas chambers and crematoria for disposing of the remains.

Of approximately six million Jews murdered in the Holocaust, more than half were exterminated in the gas chambers or crematoriums at the Nazi Death Camps between 1942 and 1945.

We did not find out about the great number of suicides until after the war through the Red Cross. In the meantime my parents and their friends were filled with worry and dread about what was happening to the Jews left behind in Germany.

I was lucky to be given a normal upbringing in England, until the blitz started in real earnest in September 1940, with the strategic bombing of Britain and Northern Ireland until May 1941.

We children actually enjoyed some aspects of it because, as soon as the air raid siren sounded at night, we all congregated downstairs in the house, with people taking it in turns to bring us tea and biscuits. It felt like we were having an impromptu party until the 'all clear' started and we went back to our beds.

Most of our neighbours liked us and did not in any way blame us for the situation. But our lives were not without their problems, mainly due to our lack of money.

Our caretaker's daughters Maureen and Wendy asked me if we were moving out because they spotted we had no carpet in the hall. Rather than tell them that we could not afford it, I said: "No. We are still waiting for the carpet to arrive."

But that was nothing compared to the embarrassment I suffered when I accepted their invitation to have tea with them in the caretaker's lodge.

When I got there the girls had just come back from school and told me to come in. The table was all laid with food. They disappeared for a minute and when they returned they were both stark naked! I couldn't believe my eyes. They were both quite well developed, especially Maureen.

I was instructed to sit down, which I did. I looked at them and then at the food, but they did not seem to detect my discomfort. As Maureen bent across to pass me a jam tart, her boob brushed the tarts.

When they saw that I wasn't eating, Wendy asked: "Are you okay? Aren't you hungry?" So I said: "Not terribly." I was so embarrassed. I could not understand how two grown up girls, so well developed, could walk around in the nude. But the worst was to come!

There was a key in the door and their father came in. Maureen told him: "This is Margarete, my new friend!"

"Oh, nice to meet you, dear," he said. "I hope your enjoying your tea!" I looked at them all, the three of them. The girls were quite unconcerned at the father seeing them naked. My father had not seen me in the nude since I was four years old. Once he had a business friend over and he asked me if he could help me get undressed. I had replied: "No, especially not you!"

After a few minutes I said: "I think I will have to go. My mother is expecting me!" I dashed from the lodge as if I had been stung and rushed into our flat.

"Mum," I yelled. "You'll never guess what happened. Maureen and Wendy walked round the flat in the nude. They were completely naked! When their father came in they stayed like it, too! Their boobs touched the food."

My mother absolutely roared with laughter! "Perhaps they're naturists," she said. I was not sure what that meant. "Well," she explained, "There are some people who like to walk round naked."

I said: "I think it is disgusting."

After that I tried to avoid Maureen and Wendy, which was a bit difficult as they kept smiling at me and saying: "Will you come to tea again?" I had to keep making excuses.

Some people were very kind to us. I remember that one day, around Christmas 1942, we had a visit from a charming couple, a Mr. and Mrs. Whittaker, who were Quakers with a mission to help disadvantaged people. They wanted to befriend refugee families and make them welcome in a new land, so they invited us to their home for a Christmas dinner.

Mr. and Mrs. Whittaker had a beautiful house and two children who were in their twenties called Nora and John. They served up a delicious dinner, but I did not like the Christmas pudding they gave me.

Whenever I had something that tasted nasty to me, I would gobble it down very quickly to get rid of it. Upon seeing this, Mrs. Whittaker took my plate and said: "Oh, Margarete, you must have enjoyed that, let me give you some more!"

I looked helplessly at my mother. who said in her broken English: "Thank you, but I think she has had enough!

It was also in the winter of 1942 (when I was twelve years old), my mother received a letter from Morfields Eye Hospital informing her that they had a bed for me to go in and have my squint straightened. I was very nervous, especially as a horrible boy at school had told me that he knew someone who had had this operation and they put his eye in back to front, so that all he could see was the inside of his head.

Nevertheless, my mother took me to the hospital and left me there. I felt very homesick because I had never been away from my mother before and shed many a silent tear.

Early the next morning, a nurse came and gave me an injection, put me on a trolley and wheeled me into the theatre. Unfortunately, because of the war, there were no anaesthetists at the hospital and even though they deadened the pain with more injections, I could feel every stitch they put into my eye! However, I found it comforting that a very nice porter held my hand throughout the operation.

When they finished they wheeled me back to the ward. The nurse then told me that I would have to have both eyes covered for a week. She also told me not to cry because it would make my eye worse. After a while a cheerful voice called out to me. "Hi, my name is Mavis, I am having my squint straightened later today too." This cheered me up greatly and we became firm friends. After two days I was allowed out of bed. We had a great time walking around with our hands outstretched, banging into everything. Because we were the youngest people on the ward all the other patients gave us presents and chocolates and made a big fuss of us.

After a week the nurse told me that my bandages were going to come off that day. When I opened my eyes I saw this really handsome doctor whose name was Dr. Crawford. He said, "Margarete, you are my prized patient. Your eyes are absolutely dead centre.

The ward was now getting busy for Christmas. Mavis and I helped to make decorations. When the Sister of the ward told me, Margarete, I have some good news for you. When you mother comes to see you tomorrow, she can take you home.

I was heartbroken. I did not want to go home. I wanted to stay and enjoy the Christmas there. I was very quite on our journey home. And when we arrived in our flat, my horrible cousin Johnny was there. "Oh," He said, "Your eye looks worse than ever!" "I want to go back, I said, "I want to go back. There is no sign of Christmas here either." When my dad returned home from work, I heard him and Mum talk quietly in the hall. And I heard Mum go out to the front door. I was getting a bit worried about her then. But she returned carrying a bag from Marks and Spencer's. When I opened it I found she had bought me a beautiful grey pin striped skirt.

My eyes improved daily and before I went back to school my mother took me to the hairdresser and I had the ends of my hair very lightly permed. When the new terms started I went back to school with my head held high and actually got some wolf whistles from the boys. I said to the boy who said that my eye would be put in inside out, "You were wrong what you told me, and I now see what an ugly mug you are!"

The process of having the eye done gave me a tremendous amount of confidence, because I seemed to turn from an ugly duckling to swan!

CHAPTER 12:

FINDING WORK

In the summer of 1944 I left school at the age of 14 without any qualifications whatsoever. Some of the brighter pupils in my class took matriculation exams, which were the equivalent of today's GCSEs. If I had stayed at school I would probably had passed in English.

Although I had not been really happy at my last school, I cried, along with many of my fellow pupils, on the final day. We embraced each other and swore everlasting friendship, which, of course, never happened.

The big question now was which career should I follow? I knew that I wanted to look after children, but in order to start training for nursery nursing I had to be 16. So my father suggested that I take a shorthand and typing course which he said would always come in handy.

I duly enrolled at the evening classes of Park Lane School which was a disaster from start to finish. As I had very bad coordination, I could only type with two fingers. While my class mates were touch typing, I laboriously hit my poor type-writer with these two fingers; perspiration pouring down my face! And I found shorthand was even worse. The shorthand letters are very much like drawing and I never could draw. I was unable to read my shorthand back, and neither could anyone else! So halfway through the term, much to the relief of the teacher, who felt that I dragged the standard of the class down, I could not stand it any longer and left!

Now I was back to square one trying to decide how to fill in the next two years before I could start my 'nursery nurse' training. Then my father suddenly remembered that while he was interned in the Isle of Man he made friends with the brother of Anna Freud, who ran a residential nursery in Hampstead. My father wrote to him and got a reply quite quickly, saying that his sister would be pleased to see me.

Shaking with nerves, I went with my mother to meet the daughter of the world famous psychiatrist Sigmund Freud. We arrived at a house, which was like a mansion in the best part of Hampstead, and we were ushered into a large airy room, filled ceiling to floor with books, apart from a beautiful mahogany desk and chair. After a few moments the door opened and Anna came in.

She had quite a young face and her greying hair was tied up in a bun. She was wearing a long, flowing skirt and a blouse of the same material. After talking to my mother for a little, she turned to me and said: "Tell me, dear, why do you want to look after children?"

I knew that my answer would determine whether she'd take me on or not, so I thought for a moment before replying: "I have always loved babies and young children. All our neighbours let me look after their young children when I was still at school, and ever since I can remember this has been the one thing I have wanted to spend my life doing."

"Well," she said, "You are very young, but I will give you a month's trial in my nursery in Finchley Road. We will pay you ten shillings a week, (which today is 50 pence!), and you can start next week."

On my first day I was introduced to a woman called Sister Gertrude. She told me I was to work with the junior toddlers, aged between one and two. She took me into the room where the children were and they all looked at me with hostility. So Sister said to me: "Just ignore them. Sit on the floor and start building a tower with these bricks."

When I had put about six bricks together a beautiful little boy came over to me, knocked the bricks down and went off. I carried on with my building skills and one by one the children, (there were six of them), came over and knocked the towers down.

Eventually they sat down next to me, which resulted in me spending most of the morning building my tower and having it knocked down! One little girl got carried away with the situation, picked up a brick and threw it at my face. It struck me on the nose! Undeterred, I carried on with my task and by the end of the morning the children were all sitting round me smiling and calling out: "More bricks! More bricks!"

Sister said: "Well done, Margarete, but now it is time for lunch." This was quite an eye opener for me because the children each sat at individual tables, and a young woman came into the room pushing a trolley on which there were six little trays. I sat watching in amazement as each child had a different choice of food combinations. One little girl ate a sponge cake, dipped in gravy, while another child had mash potato with custard. A little boy threw most of his food on the floor.

After this hilarious lunch was over, the children ran amok because they did not want their faces to be wiped. Sister told me that this was a research project, looking into the eating habits of children. As the children were left to their own devices, it was thought that they would never develop eating problems.

Following lunch, the children had a rest on their little camp beds. We spent the afternoon in the garden where there was a sandpit and lots of other bits of equipment. Then it was time for their evening baths.

Finally, the children were carried down to an air raid shelter in a cellar where they were put into beds secured with nets so they couldn't fall out. I went home feeling tired but happy because I had really enjoyed my first day there.

Now I would like to describe the six children. First there was Leon, a beautiful wee boy, whose mother worked in the home. A little girl called Lydia, very blonde with a turned up nose, was the last one to make friends with me, while Margaret was a quiet red-haired girl and Alexandra was a beautiful black girl who was very intelligent. Then there was Sandy, with a mop of ginger hair. Last, but not least, was a little boy called Jimmy, who for some unknown reason spent all day in his cot.

CHAPTER 13:

TOLD TO COOK FOR 30

I loved being with the children and couldn't wait to get to work every morning. The little ones soon became very friendly and let me wash and bath them.

I knew that this was going to be my vocation. It was all I ever wanted to do. But, as I was so young and very shy, I didn't really make friends with any of the other staff. Consequently, when we all filed in for our lunch in a very big kitchen I just sat and ate my meal without saying anything to anybody.

Then I made a big mistake. One morning when I came into work Sister Gertrude said to me: "Margarete, I have some really good news. We are going to take out a group of children to our country house in Essex for about two months. You'll love it there. It is surrounded by beautiful countryside."

I was taken aback by this news because I had never been away from home before. Although I smiled at Sister and said: "Oh good!", I was filled with a sudden panic at the thought of leaving my parents, and that nobody would talk to me there, either.

When I told my parents about my offer they thought that I should go. They said that it would be good for me. I just didn't know what to do. I spent a sleepless night weighing up the pros and cons and, by the morning, decided that I wouldn't go. I rang Sister Gertrude and gave her the excuse that my parents didn't want me to spend two months away.

Her voice was quite cold when she said: "Alright then, we will ring you when we get back." The minute I made that decision I regretted it bitterly. I spent the next few weeks waiting anxiously while looking after neighbours' children. I had the sneaky feeling that they would not want me back. But, to my great relief, I received a phone call after about three weeks telling me to return to work.

When I arrived at the nursery Sister told me that they had bought four children from the country house back with them. In the big play room I immediately noticed a small boy of about 18 months old sitting on the floor doing absolutely nothing. He was beautiful to look at and I just fell in love with him.

The first day I managed to get him to play with me a little bit. The next morning when I arrived he was still in his cot, but he gave me a little smile and put his arms up. I potty trained him and gradually got him to walk. As he grew in confidence he began to interact with the other children. I adored this little boy whose name was Daniel.

On my days off I took Daniel out and bought him a pair of little sandals with my clothing coupons.

Then came another blow. I received a phone call from Sister Gertrude asking me if I had ever suffered from Scarlet Fever. I told her I hadn't. She said that there was an outbreak amongst the children and, as I had not had it before, it wouldn't be wise for me to come to work until the quarantining was over.

I was desolate. I was sure that Daniel would forget me during the time I was away. Three weeks later I was told that everything was clear and I could go back to work. With a shaking heart, I entered the nursery's play room and walked up to Daniel. As soon as he saw me he raised his arms to be picked up and wouldn't leave me all day.

On the rare occasion that Daniel's mother would

come to visit he would cling to me and cry as I tried to leave the room.

One day I had a call from Anna Freud, asking me to come and see her. I had no idea what it was about and I thought maybe it was to praise me for being so good with Daniel. But what she said was like a bolt from the blue.

She told me: "Margarete, we have bought some staff down from our house in Essex so unfortunately we don't need you any more."

"Do you want me to leave?" I asked in a shaky voice. "Well, we have a vacancy in our kitchen," Miss Freud replied. I wasn't very keen on becoming a kitchen hand, but I agreed and thought I would still be able to look after Daniel in my spare time.

Working in the big kitchen was one of the best things I ever did. I learned a lot about catering, and enjoyed the company of the other girls in the kitchen who were so friendly and jolly working under the guidance of the head cook.

I still managed to see Daniel in the morning and give him his breakfast before starting my duties. I would then skip lunch to be with him.

The motherly cook, who was called Mrs. Hart, noticed that I wasn't eating and became very concerned about my health. She made me have a small lunch before I dashed off to be with 'my little boy'.

One morning when I arrived at work, I was told: "Margarete, Mrs. Hart is off sick so you'll have to cook the lunch."

"Me, cook for 30 people?!", I said, alarmed. But I was given the blunt answer: "Well, you will have to because nobody else can." So I got to work. My wartime experiences as a member of a Jewish family battling against the odds had taught me to believe that nothing was impossible.

I put huge joints of lamb in the oven and boiled the potatoes before popping them in the oven as well. I then cooked the vegetables. At the same time I made custard in a huge double saucepan, as I had been shown, as well as a mixture for a large sponge pudding. By one o'clock the first staff sitting came for their lunch. Meanwhile, I had made a lovely thick gravy, and the girls and I took the lunch into the dining room.

I stood in the doorway and heard someone say: "This gravy is delicious, and look at these lovely crunchy potatoes! Mrs. Hart excelled herself today!" So Peggy, my special friend in the kitchen, went through and announced to everyone: "Mrs. Hart is sick today, so Margarete cooked the whole lunch, including the pudding." I was quite embarrassed when she called me into the room and everyone applauded.

All the nurses congratulated me, patting me on the shoulder and saying that they hoped Mrs. Hart would not hurry back as they enjoyed the meal so much! Even the matron, of whom everyone was in awe, personally came down to shake my hand. She told me: "Thank you so much. You have really saved the day!"

As it happened, Mrs. Hart was ill for quite a long time and there were doubts as to whether she would come back to work. So the matron asked me whether I would consider running the kitchen for a rise of five shillings a week. I agreed, mainly because I wanted to be near Daniel. I did this job until 1945 when the war came to an end.

Miss Freud began to close the nursery down. Some lucky children went back to their parents and others to care homes. Daniel, who by this time was nearly three years old, went back to France with his mother.

It took me a long time to get over missing him. But I knew in my heart that his parents really did love him. Daniel's father, who was in the French navy, was due to come home. Together they could hopefully give him a good life. Daniel's mother corresponded for a time, but then we lost contact. I have never forgotten Daniel. It is hard to believe that he is now 69 and quite possibly a grandfather.

I also wondered what happened to a little girl called Margaret, about whom a very moving film was made at the nursery in 1941 called 'Journey for Margaret'.

It was the story of a young orphan, beautifully played by a five-year-old actress called Margaret O'Brien. The little girl, also named Margaret, had lost her family in an air raid and was bought to Anna Freud by a foster carer who said that he could do nothing with her.

Apparently, Margaret was clutching an imitation bomb in one hand and wiping her eyes with the other one. Miss Freud bent over to her and said: "Do you want to cry, dear?"

The little girl answered: "You won't smack me if I scream?"

"Miss Freud told her: "No, go ahead." And the little girl began to cry with the most heartbroken sobs.

An American reporter, who was working in England at the time, heard of Margaret's plight. He took her, and another little orphan, back to America with him to live with him and his wife.

This happened before I went to work at the nursery, but the film made such an impact on me that, 70 years later, I can still visualize it as if it were yesterday.

CHAPTER 14:

AFTER THE WAR

At last the long and terrible war was over and we went back to our normal lives. Servicemen came home, but unfortunately many bereaved families had no loved one returned to them.

It was hard to believe that we were no longer in fear of flying bombs, air raids and rockets. Children went to school in the morning secure in the knowledge that their homes would be intact and their parents safe on their return.

In the spring of 1946, at the age of 16, I began my training as a nursery nurse probationer in a council-run day nursery. And what an eye opener that was.

The matron in charge was a cold and bitter woman who unfortunately had lost her own child to meningitis some years previously and I think she never really came to terms with this tragedy.

Her No. 2 was a slightly eccentric sister who would dress like a nurse, wearing a long white headdress. She was a chain smoker and used to change the babies' nappies with the ash of a cigarette getting longer and longer, but somehow or other it never dropped onto the babies. The difference between how these children were treated and how the children were looked after in Anna Freud's nursery was quite amazing. And I found it very hard to accept this.

On my first morning I found myself again working with toddlers aged between 18 months and three years old. One woman came in with a little boy called Peter. As she started to leave, he began to cry so I picked him up and took him to the window where his mother was waiting and waving. Although he was crying bitterly, he waved backed to her. I was also in tears.

Nurseries are wonderful places for children over three. Not little ones who have no conception of time, and think that when their mothers have gone they will never see them again.

At this day nursery, the babies under a year old were regularly tied to a potty stand so they would learn to be clean and dry, which was ridiculous. Children under the age of two have no control over their bladder or bowel. In fact, early potty training can do them a lot of harm psychologically. I believe in the words of a well known psychiatrist who said: "Better a dirty child, than a mentally constipated adult."

The only redeeming feature of my time there was that, instead of going to lectures after work, we were on day release. For two days a week we attended the North West Polytechnic in Camden Town, much to the disgust of the matron!

The lectures were wonderful. We learnt elementary anatomy and physiology, child psychology and how to recognise children's feelings through art. The only problem was that I was unable to practise what I learned at the polytechnic. It seemed the people who ran the nursery had no idea of child psychology. I got more and more frustrated.

I made lots of friends amongst the fellow students, and was particularly friendly with a girl called Barbara Edwards. She was a very intelligent girl who loved music, and we went to the proms together, as well as dancing regularly at the Polish and Czechoslovakia Friendship Society.

I introduced Barbara to my other friends, including a

young Jewish man called John Simons. He desperately wanted to become a doctor, but was just not able to pass any of the exams. He ended up working in a Lyon's corner house. To cut a long story short John and Barbara got married and had a little boy, but unfortunately we gradually lost touch with one another.

When I was placed to look after older children, aged from three to five, I worked with a nursery school teacher called Miss Stevens, whose ideas were similar to mine. We used to take the poorest and dirtiest children, wash them and put them into clean clothes. We spent a long time talking to them and getting them involved in different activities. It was very gratifying to see how they flourished under our care.

Whenever one works with children, it is almost impossible not to have a special rapport with them. I got quite attached to a little blonde boy called Derek Guy. I became friendly with his mother who asked me to tea at her house. She was a single mother and quite hard up so I used to take cakes with me. Mrs. Guy was a lovely young woman and did her very best to give her little boy whatever she could.

Some of the women staff at the nursery had very different outlooks. Firstly, there was Nurse Zackaman, a fellow refugee who had come to England from Germany and sadly had to leave her family behind.

She was very lonely and tried to find comfort in the local synagogue, but apparently felt she had little in common with the people, although they were Jewish, of course. So she went to the local church where the congregation welcomed her with open arms and she became an ardent born-again Christian. What was not so good was that she tried to convert everyone to Christianity! But she was a good natured soul and very fond of the children.

Then there was Helga, another German-Jewish girl who had come to England with her parents and younger brother. Her parents were comfortably off and had a luxury flat in Hampstead. Unfortunately, Helga had failed her nursery nurses exam, much to the dismay of her mother who openly showed preference for Helga's brother Claude because he was extremely clever.

I invited Helga to my home for dinner and after the meal she proceeded to show my parents and myself her gymnastic skills. She did a couple of handstands and cartwheels, practically bringing the furniture down in our small room! My Dad tactfully said: "Well done, Helga!" My mother and I looked at each other and raised our eyebrows in disbelief.

I also got to know a lot about Nurse Titchmarsh, affectionately known as Titch. She had teeth that stuck out and a very big bosom which threatened to burst through her uniform!

She confided in me when we got better acquainted that she was madly in love with her uncle and he with her. She told me how they secretly kissed in corners, hoping that Titch's parents would not see them. This was an eye opener to me as to how some older people carried on with their love lives.

There was also a small woman staff nurse called Nurse Woods, who reminded me of a witch in some respects. Her favourite remark to me was: "Nurse Mendelsohn: powers of observation nil." This she said to me whenever I missed a small mark on the table that I polished.

She was very harsh with the children. She made one little girl sit at the table with a lunch she didn't want to eat until it was nearly time for her mother to come and fetch her home. During the afternoon, when all the other children were playing – and this poor little soul was crying into her congealed food – I managed to take the plate away and put the contents into a bin.

I told Nurse Woods that she had eaten it! Nurse Woods gave me a very searching look as if she did not believe me. I had a strong desire to slap her, which, of course, I didn't as it would have cost me my job and I would have been up for assault.

A couple of months later another Jewish girl joined the staff. Her name was Erica, who had bright red hair and a colourful personality to match. She didn't give a damn for authority, but just did what she thought was best - and everyone respected her.

Erica was horrified to discover that a young girl like me had no social life and hardly went out. So she took me in hand, introduced me to her friends and suddenly I found I was going out every weekend.

The day of my examinations arrived. We had three exams: oral, practical and theoretical. My father took me to the Royal Sanitary Institute in London where the oral and theoretical tests went quite well, I thought.

For the practical exam I had to go to a strange nursery and bath and feed a red-faced, screaming baby, who was not too keen on being washed by someone he didn't know.

When I finished all these tests my dear old dad was waiting outside for me with a big ice-cream cone in one hand and an apple in the other to calm my shattered nerves.

I had to wait a month for the results. One morning Matron called me into the office and said: "Nurse Mendelsohn, you have passed your exams. A certificate will be sent to you in due course."

I felt elated and stood in front of her with a wide

grin on my face, expecting her to congratulate me. But all she said was: "Thank-you, go back to your work now!"

The other members of staff were very pleased for me, especially Miss Stevens, the nursery school teacher who had become my strongest ally.

CHAPTER 15:

DEALING WITH A DRUNKEN EMPLOYER

After working at the nursery for three years, I decided to gain some experience in the private sector. I went to an agency and had no problems in getting a job.

The women in the agency told me that I should not let people take advantage and treat me like a glorified housekeeper. She said I should make it clear from the beginning that I was a trained nursery nurse and was there only to look after the children.

My first job was with a Jewish family who had two children: a boy and a girl, aged five and three. My hours were from nine in the morning to half past five in the afternoon. The parents were very pleasant and the children were sweet, but after I had been there for a couple of weeks they asked me whether I could stay on later and look after the children while they went to a party.

I willingly agreed to do this, never dreaming that they would take advantage by not coming home all night without even phoning to warn me! So I rang my parents to say that I would be staying the night and laid down on the settee in the lounge. I didn't sleep because I was worried about the young couple in case they had had an accident.

They arrived home at ten o'clock the following morning, expecting me to stay on and look after the children during the day while they went to bed to catch up on their missed sleep. I did so, but, after consulting the agency, I gave them a week's notice, despite them begging me to stay.

As I was leaving, I asked them why they did not have the courtesy to ring me. Their feeble reply was that they could not find a telephone!

My next job was with a rather posh lady living in a mansion near Hyde Park. She had four children: two boys at boarding school and two little ones called Mary and Edward who were going to be in my care. She was divorced from her husband, an important figure in the media world who had re-married and hardly saw his children.

I had been there about a week when she came home drunk one evening and passed out. I had no choice but to cover her with a blanket and stay the night to look after the children. I thought that maybe this was a 'one off' and that she was depressed. As the children became very attached to me and the pay was excellent I decided not to tell the agency and to stay on.

But she came home drunk nearly every night. On one occasion she was sick and vomited everywhere. I felt that enough was enough and gave her a month's notice.

I was concerned about the children, and telephoned her ex-husband to inform him of the situation. He told me he couldn't look after them himself so he intended to put them in a foster home. It was very sad.

After I left this job I debated whether to go back to nursery work, but decided to have one more try in the hope that I would find a relatively sober family!

I was rewarded with the best job that I ever had. It was with Mr. and Mrs. Henry and their four children, who lived in a large house in Norland Square, Kensington. The children were Michael, who was at St. Paul's School, six-year-old Silvia, (affectionately known as Tootsie because she was so small), four-year-old Anna, a blonde beauty with a temper, and an angelic two-year-old called Elisabeth. The youngest two were in my charge.

The children's mother was a very pretty 30-year-old called Naomi and the father Jon was a medical student whose studies had been interrupted when he was called up for the army during the war.

Naomi's parents, Mr. and Mrs. Gilbert, also resided with them. Mr. Gilbert was a solicitor and Mrs. Gilbert was a plump lady who wore a velvet beret from the time she got up in the morning until she went to bed at night. All of them were extremely kind to me, and I became particularly fond of Naomi because she was only about eight years older than me and we spent a lot of time chatting.

The Henrys came to dinner at our flat. My mother cooked a delightful meal of fricassee of chicken, followed by one of her special apple cakes with whipped cream. The young couple thoroughly enjoyed the evening and invited us all to a dinner-dance at an up-market restaurant in London to which I brought along my then boyfriend Jim as well as my parents.

The Henrys were extremely generous and took me with them when they went on holiday to the seaside resort of Bexhill.

I stayed with the Henrys for three years until Anna was ready for school and little Elizabeth went to a playgroup. They wanted me to care for the children in the holidays and pick them up from school, but that wasn't quite enough for me and I got a job in a home for unmarried mothers and babies.

Working in this home was a very rewarding experience. At times it was heartbreaking when young mothers had to give up their babies, but I was able to share the joy of those whose families supported them and let them take their children home.

I can honestly say that amongst all the young mothers we had there was not one who did not care about the fate of their unborn child.

The home was run for the Red Cross by a wonderful woman who was happily married and had two grown up children.

Young women would come to us six weeks before their babies were due. They went to hospital to give birth and then returned to the home for a further three months. They all breast fed their babies for the first four weeks and bonded with them, knowing that they may soon have to part with them.

It used to make my blood boil when one or two of the girls' mothers came to see the babies and drooled over them, but were too embarrassed about what their neighbours might think to take their daughters and their little ones home to care for them.

I will never forget the adoption process. The unmarried mothers had spent the morning dressing their babies in the little outfits they had bought them. They then sobbed bitterly as they had to leave their babies. In contrast, the adopters were absolutely in raptures as many had tried to have their own children but could not. After a few tips from the sister they took the babies home.

My job was to comfort the grieving birth mothers, although all I could do was put my arm round them and cry as well. This was particularly painful for me because I had taught them how to make up bottles and sterilise them, how to bath the babies and generally to care for them. I could hardly bare to think of the grief the mothers must have felt at losing their babies. I went home many a night and cried my eyes out.

I can vividly remember when I later met one of the young mothers who had given up her child. She was walking along the street with a lost and forlorn expression on her face. She had her arms crossed as though she was cuddling an imaginary baby.

But I also witnessed a few joyful experiences. One occurred when, just before a young mother's baby was due to be handed over to adopters, a young man rushed through the door, accompanied by his parents, and took mother and child home with them.

There were some other happy reunions. I remember one Jewish girl who knew from the onset of her pregnancy that her mother and father would love and support her. The parents came to take her and her baby home.

CHAPTER 16:

HEART-BREAK AND GETTING THE SACK

During this time I went to a tea dance in a very nice hall called the Astoria. There, for two shillings and six pence, (or 30p in today's money), you could dance for two hours and have a coffee and a biscuit thrown in!

One afternoon a young, good looking red-haired man asked me to dance. We spent the rest of the afternoon together and arranged to meet the following day outside the new theatre at Baker Street.

He arrived wearing the uniform of an RAF Lieutenant and looking absolutely devastating. He held my hand in the cinema and said he wanted to see the film all over again because he so liked the feel of my hand in his.

The young man's name was Ray and he came from Yorkshire. We began to see each other regularly and I took him home to dinner to meet my parents. He arrived at our flat carrying a large bunch of flowers for my mother and a bottle of whisky for my dad.

My parents thought Ray was charming and they could see how happy he made me. I was with him for two years during which I had a wonderful time, going to dances and functions at the officer's mess.

I met his best friend Jack and Jack's wife Molly, with whom we did lots of things together as a foursome.

As Ray began to suffer from vertigo he resigned from the air force and got a job as a maths teacher in a grammar school. My world fell apart when I discovered that he was a womaniser and had been lying to me. Our parting was inevitable but it greatly upset me.

Myself age 22, Wembly Park.

It was a difficult period in my life as things also went wrong for me when I decided to try my hand at other types of work. I got a job in a factory where they made silver foil. Unfortunately, as I was not very good with my hands, my rolls of foil always seemed to come out very creased.

But the worst thing was that as we had to clock in with a time card as we arrived in the morning and I somehow always clocked in with someone else's card. So by the end of the week various unlucky members of staff found a great discrepancy in their wages! As I was afraid of being lynched I quickly resigned.

Then I got a job as an assistant in a chemist shop and that also ended in disaster. I could never remember where everything was! Once, in my haste to get a bottle of cough medicine off the shelf, my sleeve caught in a few empty bottles which smashed on to the floor! The chemist looked at me with venom and muttered the words "You're fired!"

Undeterred, I thought 'third time lucky'. I was taken on at Woolworths as a temporary assistant in the handkerchief department. I enjoyed folding up hankies and putting them into bags for the customers, but I never quite came to grips with the cash register. I either gave customers too much change or not enough.

After a few weeks the supervisor told me that I was not really cut out for the job so, with a great sigh of relief, I left. I decided that I preferred working with children.

However, my parents were trying to build up a retail handbag and leather goods business and asked me if I would be interested in working for them for a time. This offer appealed to me because I knew my parents would not be cross with me if I gave the wrong change.

Next to looking after children this turned out to be one of the most enjoyable experiences in my working life.

Our first venture was in Watford market. The other stall holders were very interesting. Directly opposite us was a little man who sold curtains. He was a chain smoker and said he woke up at six in the morning, coughed until seven and then had a cigarette. That was the only cigarette he lit with his lighter all day because he then continuously lit one from the other. He was very funny and the customers seemed to like him.

Next to him was a stall called 'Joe for Jeans'. The bloke who ran the stall did so well that at the end of the day he literally had three paper bags full of money. I thoroughly enjoyed it because there were lots of young men to flirt with, and often I went to coffee with one or two of them. My father had to remind me I was supposed to be working!

We then branched out and took a corner shop in a covered market in Slough. My mother also came to serve in the shop which we called 'Sally Stores'. Opposite us was a Mr. Collins, an 80-year-old butcher. He had an employee called Bill whose nose was always dripping. He spent all day cutting up horse meat which was supposed to be delicious, but I never fancied tasting any of it.

Our business went from strength to strength and my father began to sell trunks and very expensive leather goods. We had no car, because dad never learned to drive, so all our stock came in by rail.

In terms of my relationships over years that followed I went out with various young men. I met an Israeli Jewish accountant called Maurice who seemed very nice. We started going out together and four months into the relationship I discovered that I was pregnant.

They say history repeats itself, but my position was quite different to my poor Aunt Margarete. When I told my parents about my predicament they supported me with love and devotion.

On July 6th 1957 my first son David Anthony was born. He was the apple of my parents' eye and the son my father never had. My dad loved to take David out in the beautiful silver pram they had bought for him and stood by proudly while the neighbours admired the lovely baby.

David, unable to say "Granddad", called him "Dad-dad" and to all intents and purposes my dad was his father, too. David turned our little flat into a wonderland of toys and baby powder. Although both my parents idolised him, they didn't spoil him or interfere with my way of bringing him up. People called David the Prince of Empire Court because of the beautiful clothes he had.

Then something unexpected happened. When David was 18 months old, we had a visit from an elderly Israeli man who told us that he was David's father's uncle. Apparently Maurice's family in Egypt were aware of David's existence and were quite upset that they had no contact with him.

The uncle said that Maurice would like to see his son, but, as he did not want to come to our flat, he suggested that we met briefly at Wembley Park station. So on a cold winter's morning I bundled David into his pram and walked up to the station where Maurice was waiting, holding a present under his arm. He went up to David and proceeded to lift him out of his pram.

I thought that David would cry because he was shy with strangers. But he took Maurice's finger and they both walked up the road together. I must admit I felt quite emotional and realised that blood is thicker than walker. After that Maurice came to visit me regularly at home when my parents were at work. But my father was so scared that Maurice might abduct David that he asked my Aunt Martha to be there as a chaperone.

After a few weeks Maurice wanted to take David and myself to Egypt, but I did not like the idea and declined his offer. If we had gone with him it would have broken my parents' hearts.

We kept in touch by letter for sometime and then lost contact. I stupidly did not keep any of the photos of Maurice and me together. So David had no idea what his father looked like until he managed to find him and meet him many years later.

Sadly, both my parents died before David gained a degree in Peace Studies in July 1987. But on the day of his graduation from Bradford University, as my daughter Francesca and I were about to leave for Bradford, a letter arrived for me, as the executor of my mother's will.

It contained a five pound postal order, and it was as though his grandparents were saying, "sorry we couldn't be with you today but you know how proud we are."

As my son mounted the steps in the hall of the university to receive his 2:1 degree, I could see that under his gown he was wearing a very shabby tweed jacket, and he told me later that he graduated wearing his granddad's jacket and tie.

When David was three I met a Jewish man called Len, who had a 10-year-old daughter, Yvonne. I wasn't madly in love with Len, but he was very likeable and witty. David and Yvonne immediately became very close and she was like another mother to him.

I married Len in January, 1961 and a year later

my second son Jonathan was born. He had a fuzz of ginger hair and was always hungry!

Within another 18 months I gave birth to my daughter Francesca, who is named after my father's mother. And four years later, to the day on August 24th, my youngest son Simon was born in 1967. It was quite odd having two children on the same date.

Simon's was the quickest birth of all, and when the midwife held him up she said she would not buy a chicken that size! But he grew into a beautiful boy.

Now, at the age of 82, I have got four loving and supportive children, two wonderful grandchildren, Amy and Michael, and a three-year-old great granddaughter, Isabella.

Unfortunately, things didn't work out between Len and I, although we were happy at the beginning. So, after 25 years I was compelled to end the marriage. But I am so happy to have such a wonderful family, and keep counting my blessings!

My great granddaughter
Isabella in 2012

My grandson Michael and daughter
Francesca

CHAPTER 17:

PLAGUED BY DEPRESSION

I very often think how much I owe to my lovely parents because, without their foresight and resolution to leave everything behind in Berlin and get us to safety to this wonderful England, none of us would be here today.

The terrible atrocities that occurred in Germany are as real to me now as if they had happened yesterday. The horrors have never left me.

Immediately after my first son David was born I had recurring nightmares of being chased by unseen footsteps as I ran, holding him in my arms. Just when we were about to be caught, I woke up bathed in a cold sweat, with my heart beating like a sledge hammer.

I spent the whole night cradling my baby in my arms, stroking his face, and finding it hard to believe that he and I were safe in our warm bed, with my parents near by.

All through my adult life I have suffered bouts of depression, which have been partly due to the traumas and fear I experienced as a young, impressionable child when my mother and I were stuck in Berlin.

Living in Nazi Germany was bad enough, but learning from the Red Cross after the war that many Jews had poisoned their children first and then themselves to escape the concentration camps was just as devastating.

It had a terrible effect on my parents and myself to think that some of our relatives and friends had been so fearful that they had decided to take this tragic step.

As I was only a child when we left Germany, my recollection of them was quite scanty, but I was naturally appalled at this news.

In my vivid imagination I could see my uncles and aunts putting their children to bed with a goodnight kiss and giving them a spoonful of arsenic. Then they would have taken a dose themselves and all died together.

As I said earlier, my grandmother Francisca had been arrested at the age of 78 and taken to a concentration camp called Theresienstadt. According to the Red Cross, this camp was not as severe as Auschwitz, but she died a year after she was imprisoned. The cause of her death was unexplained.

My father was devastated to hear of the terrible treatment and ultimate death of his mother. I was extremely upset, too, even though I was not as close to her as I was to my other grandmother.

The thought of her being taken screaming from her flat and then driven off in a police van to be locked up has haunted me for most of my life. Since writing this autobiography some of these thoughts have come to the foreground.

My first bad depression came after my father Alfred died. My mother at that time was already senile so, as an only child, I had to arrange my father's funeral, obtain a death certificate and put his affairs in order. Consequently I had no time to grieve for him.

I spent the next six months after my father's death travelling to London to be with my mother three times a week, ensuring she had 'meals on wheels' which she did not really want. Then I would go back home to Brighton to work and be with my children.

Suddenly I felt that I would not cope very well. I suffered a deep depression and briefly went into a rest home where I was put on medication.

These bouts of depression have followed me through the years. So sometimes they come without any explanation and at other times have been triggered by a family problem or worry.

I have read and heard of lots of other people who also have had some form of mental ill health due living at such a traumatic time as Nazi Germany.

Even when we were safety in England my mother had very bad panic attacks, due to what she had been through in Germany and having to leave her mother behind. After the devastating news that Grandma Tony had died, my mum went into a very deep depression and my father and I felt unable to help her.

CHAPTER 18:

MY MOTHER AND FATHER

My mother Selli was born 1902 and was bought up by my grandparents, who owned a department store and a farm in a small garrison town of Arys in East Prussia. She was a bright, beautiful girl and the apple of her father's eye.

Selli's sister Martha was a year older, but very shy. When Martha was due to start school she refused to go unless her sister went with her, so little Selli sat at the back of the class and was spoilt by everybody.

Their father was an orthodox Jew and was worried that his girls might end up marrying one of the officers stationed in Arys.

He sent his two daughters to an exclusive finishing school in Berlin. There, at a tea dance, Selli met and fell in love with a Jewish doctor in his early 30's. When she bought him home her father disliked him because he felt the doctor was big headed. Her father made enquires about the man's background and learned that he was living with an older woman who was subsidizing him because his practice had failed.

Upon hearing about this, Selli went into a deep depression, spoke to no one and just spent hours walking her faithful Alsatian called Witan. She hardly ate anything and lost a lot of weight so her father arranged for her to stay with relations in Berlin. Once there, she gradually perked up a little, and at a party met a young, pleasant looking, red-haired man called Alfred Mendelsohn, who was to become my father.

Alfred, apparently not the type of man my mother had previously gone out with, was kind and generous, showering her with red roses every week. He took her to concerts, operas and tea dances, and when he proposed to her she accepted.

Selli's parents admired the fact that the young man was sincere, hard working, and in the process of opening a lucrative advertising agency with the help of his father Moritz.

My aunt Margarete, uncle Gustav and father
as children in Berlin

When Alfred took Selli home to meet his family, his brother Gustav and father immediately took a shine to her, but his mother Francisca didn't like her. She thought that Selli was too well dressed and too worldly wise, and her relationship with my mother never improved in all the years my parents were married.

They married in January 1929, and I was born a year later.

I now turn to my father's early life. When he and his two siblings were very young, my grandparents Moritz and Francisca were struggling financially. My grandfather tried his hand at many different ventures, but nothing seemed to work. In desperation he went to America where he had some relations who had promised to help him.

Meanwhile, my grandmother worked at home, addressing envelopes for a mail company until late at

My grandmother Francisca and
my beloved grandfather Moritz 1934

night in very bad light, which permanently impaired her eyesight.

Moritz found that the streets of New York were not paved with gold, but, after returning home, he managed to obtain a job as a clerk and his fortunes improved.

When Dad reached the age of 25 he and my grandfather went into business together and built up their advertising agency which they called it Menso & Son. They rented a room in a house and began sending out letters, seeking advertising orders from businessmen.

Alfred travelled round Germany to make more contacts and after a couple of years the business really took off. This resulted in them employing about 30 workers.

My dear father found working in England difficult, not least because of his problems with the language.

Once when he was visiting a lady customer to sell her leather goods she told him how she was struggling to survive on her own because her husband was very ill. So he took her hand and said: "Madam, I adore you!"

He was taken aback when she became very cold towards him and cancelled her order. He told me about this, and I explained that he should have said: "Madam, I admire you."

I telephoned the lady on his behalf and she broke into fits of laughter when I told her what he had meant to say. It really cheered her up and she gave my father more orders for leather goods.

When my father had to introduce himself to people he just met and introduced himself as Alfred Mendelsohn, the first reaction of the other people was, 'Oh, are you any relation to the great composer?' And with a very serious face my father would reply, 'Yes our grandmothers were brothers!' The people then would nod and smile and walk on. My father would then watch as they stood still in their tracks realising they had been hoodwinked. Whether we actually are related to the composer we will never know (the spelling is different).

All we know is my aunt was a gifted pianist while my son David studied piano and clarinet. My son Simon is a brilliant drummer and guitarist and my other son Jonathan was a very good actor. Also my daughter Francesca was a great dancer. I myself can play nothing but have a great appreciation for most kind of music. My father used to say, 'Music is food for the soul.

One of the other endearing memories of the things my father said was this: When I was in my teens and a lot the relationships I had went wrong, he would say to me, "never mind darling, every saucepan had a lid and you will find yours."

My father's older brother Gustav and younger sister Margarete had mixed fortunes.

Gustav was very charming and wanted to be an actor - the only trouble was that he could not act! He spent most of his time mixing with young women who were fairly well off and able to support him. But he seemed to think the grass was always greener somewhere else. So he changed his girlfriends as soon as he got fed up with them.

His mother Francisca worshipped the ground that he walked on and when he was between lady friends she supported him with the little money that she had.

In contrast to Gustav and Alfred, their sister Margarete was very talented musically, but she died tragically.

CHAPTER 19:

AUNT MARGARETE'S TRAGIC DEATH

It was not until I was in my late teens that my parents told me the truth about the death of my aunt Margarete, after whom I was named. Previously, my father had spared me the heartbreaking details by saying that it had been due to an infection of her lungs.

As a child she used to listen to classical music on the radio and move her hands up and down the table, pretending to play an imaginary piano. So my grandfather bought her a piano.

She taught herself to play, and to encourage this obvious talent my grandfather hired a music teacher. Margarete progressed so well that, after a year, her tutor said she had the makings of a child prodigy and there was nothing more he could show her. So he recommended a renowned professor of music who only taught children with exceptional ability.

In order to pay for Margarete to have lessons from the professor, my grandfather found a job as a cleaner in an office, working every night. My grandmother, who appeared to be jealous of the relationship between father and daughter, was sarcastic about Margarete's music and thought that it would never come to anything.

But soon Margarete was giving recitals, and was able to teach students to help pay for her own studies, so that my grandfather would not have to do two jobs. One of the students, a very good looking charmer called Carl, proved to be her downfall.

Carl was the first young man with whom she struck up a close friendship and they became lovers.

When Margaret told her father that she and Carl wished to get engaged, Granddad was not happy. He didn't trust the young man, who seemed too brash and sure of himself. But, as Granddad did not want to risk losing his daughter, he gave his grudging consent, even going as far as offering Carl a junior position in the company he ran with dad. Grandma told her daughter that it would all end in tears, and for once she was right.

Carl told Granddad that he must break the news of the engagement to his parents, who lived in Dresden. Margarete suggested she went with him, but Carl said his father was not too well so it was best that he went home on his own. Carl promised to telephone her as soon as he arrived in Dresden.

The call never came, and when Margarete tried to phone him she found that the number he had given her did not exist. She was sick most mornings, but assured her worried father that she was simply suffering from a tummy bug. She cancelled her students' lessons and declined an offer to give a piano recital to the annoyance of her music professor.

Margarete was actually pregnant and was ashamed to tell anyone. She was horrified of the way her mother would probably react to the news of her daughter's moral downfall.

She found the address of a private doctor who performed abortions, but apparently his attitude disgusted her and she could not bear the thought of him touching her body and the body of her unborn baby.

After agonizing for weeks, she crept out of her

home early one morning, caught a train to a seaside resort, walked into the water and drowned herself.

Granddad Moritz never really recovered from this terrible loss. His hair turned white overnight, his previously upright posture became bowed and he developed breathing difficulties. He bitterly blamed his wife for the death of their daughter. He told her that she should have been the person Margarete could have counted on for love and support without any reservation.

My poor granddad could not bring himself to look at the baby grand piano he had skimped and scraped to buy for his talented daughter. So Dad arranged for it to go into storage. After my parents were married and moved in to their apartment, the beautiful baby grand had pride of place in their lounge.

Some time later when my parents were entertaining business friends in their home, one of the guests, a young man, asked if he could play a tune on the piano. My parents looked at my grandfather, who had come to visit, and he felt obliged to agree.

The young man sat down and played a piece my aunt used to play. My grandfather's face went completely ashen and he left the room. Mum found him slumped on a chair in their bedroom sobbing as though his heart would break. He then could not catch his breath, so dad rang our doctor who came and diagnosed a severe attack of angina.

Granddad Moritz died a year later in 1937 when I was seven. The doctor diagnosed a heart attack brought on by grief, stress and trauma following his daughter's suicide. He had been further upset by the knowledge that my father and mother planned to emigrate to England.

Even though I had not inherited any of his daughter's musical talent, he loved me unconditionally, for myself.

I will always remember how he used to sit with me, listening to me read a chapter out of my school book to him. Grandma would look on with envy. I felt a bit sorry for her, but we were just not on the same wave length.

EPILOGUE:

RETURN TO BERLIN

During the summer of 1986 I returned to Berlin with my four children, David, Jonathan, Francesca and Simon.

I wanted them to see the place where I grew up for the first eight years of my life, but I felt very uncomfortable. I didn't like hearing all the German being spoken around me or having to speak German myself.

Everything I remembered about Berlin seemed the same, yet somehow different! I could not take my

My great granddaughter Isabella, daughter Francesca and granddaughter Amy in 2012

children to see the flat where I was born because at that time it was in the Eastern part.

We all enjoyed the excellent food and stayed in a very nice hotel where my aunt Hilda had rented two rooms for us. Berlin itself is a beautiful city. All the streets were spotlessly clean, with loads of cycle lanes, and anyone caught jay walking was fined on the spot. The service in the shops was amazing and customers were treated with the utmost respect by extremely helpful assistants.

I took my children to checkpoint Charlie, which was the barrier between East and West Germany, and looked at pictures of people in the East trying to escape to the West. I am afraid that I could find no sympathy for them because they were able to work and send their children to school, whereas six million of my people were sent to gas chambers.

While we were in Berlin I heard a very interesting and moving story, which was told to me by my aunt's great friend Mrs. Meyer. During her time at university around 1940 she met a young Jewish law student called Hans and they fell madly in love. Even through Mrs. Meyer's parents were high up in the Gestapo, the Nazis would have immediately ended the couple's relationship. She managed to hide her lover right through the war.

Her university friends sheltered the young man in their cellars and lofts for a short time. During the rest of the war Mrs. Meyer hid Hans in bus shelters, railway stations, stationary trains and where ever she could find a reasonable nook or cranny. She became pregnant and gave birth to a daughter in hospital, but had to put on the birth certificate 'father unknown'.

After the war, Mrs. Meyer married Hans, who finished his studies and became an eminent lawyer.

They had one more child, a son, and Mrs. Meyer was able to name the father on the boy's birth certificate.

But their daughter bore a grudge about this, and when I met her she seemed to be very bitter. Her views greatly differed from mine, and she said to me: "You should not wear your Star of David in Germany, and draw attention to yourself." My reply was: "Six million of our people died so I wear my Star of David proudly, without any fear."

Unfortunately, Hans died of a heart attack when his son was ten years old. Mr. Meyer was only in his late 30's, but the years spent in hiding had taken a great toll on his health.

I had great admiration for Mrs. Meyer's courage. She befriended my family and myself, inviting us frequently during our stay for meals at her luxury apartment. She always sent her big limo to collect us.

When she passed away two years later my aunt was devastated.

I went to Berlin on my own a further two or three times. On my second trip the German government paid for myself and other Jewish people of my generation to stay in top hotels. We went on a tour with a young Christian university lecturer who said to us: "The sins of our fathers lay heavy on our shoulders."

I also stayed with my aunt Hilda in her flat near the Kurfurstendamm, one of the most famous avenues in Berlin. I remember going out about 10pm to have a look at Berlin's night-life. It was lovely strolling past cafés, offering beautiful pastries, and people on the pavement selling arts and crafts. I felt completely safe.

This was in direct contrast to he next time I went to Berlin, just after the wall had come down, which was, I think, a big mistake as it happened too quickly for people to adjust. Everything was completely different.

There was a tense atmosphere, with petty crime rife and Turkish people and their children begging in streets and cafés. My aunt told me to keep a firm hold of my handbag and forbade me to go out in the streets at night.

On my last visit Aunt Hilda took me to a service in a Jewish house of prayer which two men were guarding. I couldn't follow the service because I was too scared and kept looking over my shoulder, but there were quite a few people in the congregation. I find it hard to understand how Jewish people can go back to live in Germany.

I know that my aunt wished she and my uncle had come to live in England when they returned from South America after the war. But the German government had offered them a good state pension which they could not refuse. Unfortunately, my aunt is now senile and living in a home so I have never been back to Berlin. In fact, I never want to step on German soil again.

This is because each time I came back to England and my plane landed at Gatwick Airport I breathed a sigh of relief at being home and was not afraid any more.

As I said in an earlier chapter, leaving my beloved grandmother behind in Germany was the hardest and saddest experience in my young life. Even now at the age of 82, the image of her standing on our balcony waving us off as we got into our taxi is as clear in my mind as if it had happened yesterday.

The experiences I had in that last year in Germany will always be in my mind, but I have moved on. My life in England is now focused on my four wonderful children, David, Jonathan, Francesca and Simon, two grandchildren Michael and Amy and delightful great granddaughter Isabelle.

I love England. Since I arrived in 1938 I had received nothing but kindness and generosity from English people and could not dream of living anywhere else.

But never a day goes by when I don't remember how lucky I was to survive the holocaust with my dear parents, who showed me such love and devotion. I am eternally grateful to my father for realising what was going to happen and getting my mother and I out of Germany, even though it meant leaving most of our possessions behind.

If he had not done so I would not be alive to tell this story. Unhappily, all his relations who thought they were immune from the trouble left it too late.

My sons David, Simon, Jonathan and me in 2012

FOOT NOTE

When I was on holiday with my friend Jackie in Chichester four years ago we walked through a market and I happened to spot a doll on a stall.

The doll was laying there with nothing on her legs and a horrible dress on. But she had almost exactly the same facial features as my old doll Hans that the Nazi youths broke when I was a child.

As I picked her up she opened her eyes and seemed to say, "please buy me."

I just could not believe it. I asked the stall holder how much she was, and willingly gave him the £2 he wanted. In fact, I would have paid ten times as much for her.

I have still got her with me now. No, I have not gone senile! I do not play with her, but it just gives me a lovely warm feeling to cuddle her soft body, dress her in pretty clothes and have her on my pillow next to me at night. I have called her Victoria. She is my victory over the Nazis.

Myself and
my doll Victoria

Lightning Source UK Ltd.
Milton Keynes UK
UKOW02f0626110516
273982UK00001B/6/P